Turkey

A TRAVELLER'S HISTORICAL AND ARCHITECTURAL GUIDE

IN MEMORY OF ALVAH HOLBERT

Turkey

A TRAVELLER'S HISTORICAL AND ARCHITECTURAL GUIDE

❧❈❧

JAMES STEELE
with photographs by ERSIN ALOK

SCORPION PUBLISHING LIMITED

NOTE ON SPELLING

Every effort has been made to use familiar and acceptable spellings of proper names. For classical placenames with their modern equivalents see the section at the end of the book.

ACKNOWLEDGEMENTS

This book owes much to the vision of Leonard Harrow whose patience and advice have made it possible. Ersin Alok unfailingly shared his time and resources, and his photographic talent has added immeasurably to the work. Aytin Öztürk of his staff offered great assistance in the selection of the photographs used, helping me to sort, organise and select what was needed from a large quantity of exceptional material, and to Ann Knudsen for her excellent work on many of the drawings. My wife, Marie, has been through each step of the progress of the book with me and deserves great credit for her understanding.
While at King Faisal University, I was assisted a great deal by both Okhan Üstinkök and Alpay Özdural on staff there, as well as by Orhan Özgüner of the King Fahad University of Petroleum and Minerals, who gave freely of their time and knowledge.
Finally, I would like to thank Dean Wayne Drummond at Texas Tech University for his encouragement during the completion of this work.

First published in 1990 by Scorpion Publishing Ltd,
Victoria House, Buckhurst Hill, Essex IG9 5ES, England

General Editor: Leonard Harrow
House Editor: John Orley
Editorial Assistant: Kay Larkin
Art Director: Colin Larkin
Designer: Andrew Nash
Production Assistant: Sue Pipe
Typeset in Linotype Melior 10 on 12 point
Colour originated by Dot Gradations Ltd
Printed on 115gsm Matt Art
Printed and bound in England by Jolly & Barber Ltd, Rugby

CONTENTS

MAP   6

INTRODUTION   7

CHAPTER I MARMARA   9

CHAPTER II THE AEGEAN COAST   47

CHAPTER III THE MEDITERRANEAN COAST   59

CHAPTER IV SOUTH EASTERN TURKEY   132

CHAPTER V THE EAST   138

CHAPTER VI CENTRAL ANATOLIA   144

CHAPTER VII THE BLACK SEA COAST   153

NOTES FOR THE TRAVELLER   158

CLASSICAL PLACENAMES WITH MODERN EQUIVALENTS   161

SELECTED BIBLIOGRAPHY   163

INDEX   164

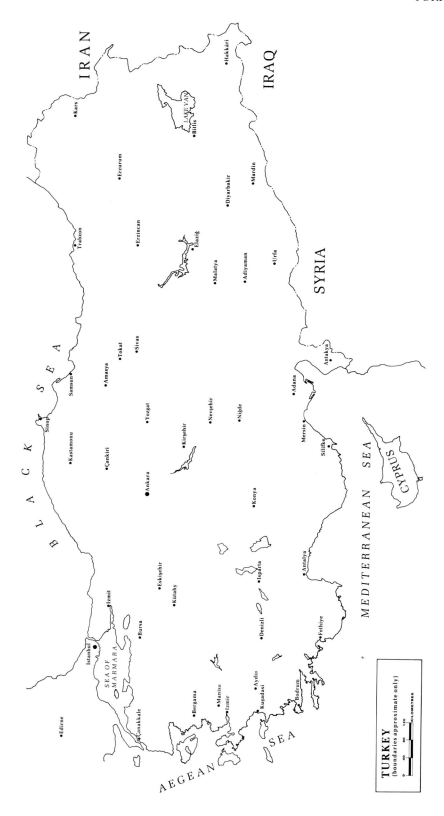

IRAN

IRAQ

•Kars

•Hakkâri

LAKE VAN

•Bitlis

•Erzurum

•Diyarbakir

•Mardin

SYRIA

•Trabzon

•Erzincan

•Elaziğ

•Malatya

•Adiyaman

•Urfa

B L A C K   S E A

•Tokat

•Sivas

•Amasya

Samsun•

•Antakya

•Adana

Sinop•

•Kastamonu

•Yozgat

•Nevşehir

•Niğde

•Çankiri

•Kirşehir

Mersin•

•Ankara

Silifke•

MEDITERRANEAN SEA

CYPRUS

•Konya

•Eskişehir

•Kütahy

•Antalya

Izmit•

•Bursa

SEA OF MARMARA

•Isparta

•Denizli

Istanbul•

•Fethiye

•Edirne

•Çanakkale

•Bergama

•Manisa

•Izmir

•Aydin

Kuşadasi•

Bodrum•

A E G E A N   S E A

TURKEY
(boundaries approximate only)

KILOMETRES

0   40   80   120

INTRODUCTION

Turkey is a country of enormous physical size, and has such a complex historical and cultural background that it would be presumptuous of anyone to attempt to contain it within a single volume. This book has instead used the concept of a journey through each of the seven geographical regions of the country, in such a way as to make it comprehensible and to arrive at a descriptive outline of its great diversity.

That journey begins in Marmara, or more specifically Istanbul, which has reflected both the conscience and soul of Turkey for such a long time. As a result of its unique topography and incremental development, Istanbul has evolved into several highly distinct neighbourhoods, which in many cases are centred around public squares. These are identified in the narrative, and described in turn, as a way of giving a clearer idea of the structure and urban pattern of this fascinating city. Other important historical centres, such as Bursa and Edirne, are also described and the key role they have had in the development of the nation is outlined.

From Marmara the journey continues on to the Aegean coast, which, from the ruins of ancient Troy in the north to Bodrum in the south, contains such a wealth of interest for the traveller. In this region that interest is inevitably focused on a classical legacy that is clearly marked out in the enormous amount of archaeological evidence remaining in cities such as Assos, Pergamon, Sardis, Ephesus, Priene, Miletus, Didyma, and many others. The important function of these cities in helping to shape the history of the Hellenic, Hellenistic, Roman and Ottoman periods provide endless opportunities for detailed study.

The Mediterranean region, which adjoins the Aegean, is the third main geographic zone of Turkey and has cleaner and more extensive beaches than any other country in the area. Because of the rugged topography of the Taurus mountains, that meander backwards and forwards toward the coast along its entire length, many of the cities built in the past in this region have remained unknown to the West until recently, and also have a highly individual character. Those nearer the coast, such as Antakya and Anemorion, have had a more pronounced Roman influence because of its extended maritime control of the Mediterranean, and provide a counterpoint to their less worldly and more remote inland cousins. That cosmopolitan character is more evident today than ever before, especially in port cities such as Bodrum, Marmaris and Antalya, whose marinas bristle with a forest of yacht masts all year long.

The atmosphere recedes quickly along the adjoining landward border with Syria and Iraq, that defines the lower edge of the south eastern region. Each of these neighbouring countries has had a significant sociological and architectural impact upon this fourth major zone of Turkey. The full extent of this influence, which can be traced to the first riverine civilizations that evolved along the banks of the Tigris and Euphrates, is clearly read in cities such as Mardin, Urfa, Diyarbakır and Hakkari. As is always the case in this country of so many historical layers, however, there are countless other cross-currents of influence that are also legible here, and these are also traced in the text.

The eastern region bordering on both Iran and the USSR is Turkey's fifth, and perhaps least travelled, area, because it is usually billed in popular journals as being accessible only to the most intrepid. That reputation is now largely unfounded, and need not dissuade those who wish to visit this hauntingly beautiful region where access is now greatly improved. Lake Van, the largest in the country, has an almost mystical attraction and is a visual as well as a literal oasis in the midst of the barren landscape that surrounds it.

From Van the course of the journey turns westward towards central Anatolia which is the heartland of the nation. The rich, fertile soil of the region, which first attracted Turkish tribes westward in search of a respite from a harsh nomadic existence on the plains of Central Asia, still covers much of the evidence of the Hittite civilization that established itself here in the past. That culture, which was one of the richest of ancient times, is only faintly echoed in the ruins of their capital at Hattuşaş, which is now called Boğazkale, or at the rock-cut gallery built to honour their thousand deities at Yazılıkaya. Cappadocia remains as a stark exception to the agricultural fertility of the rest of Anatolia, and is often described as a barren moonscape by those who do not take time to know the region better. Verdant pockets, like that of the Ihlara Gorge, totally disprove this hasty impression and prompt a more thorough exploration of this variegated landscape.

Karadeniz, or the Black Sea, is the seventh and final region to be visited, and is not exactly the reverse image of the Akdeniz, or 'White Sea' of the Mediterranean, that its name would lead one to expect. The Giresun and Karadeniz mountain chains that frame the Black Sea coast make this the 'land of mists', and the rains that fall on their seaward slopes have turned the region into a lush, cool, green paradise that has allowed tea and tobacco plantations to thrive. From Trabzon in the east, which held out as a Byzantine capital for nearly a decade after the fall of Constantinople, to the beautiful beaches of Şile in the west, this coastline is as full of surprises as Turkey itself.

CHAPTER I
MARMARA

In July of 1203, the Venetian Doge, Enrico Dandolo, led a fleet of 200 ships and 25,000 men up the Dardanelles toward Constantinople, which, as the historian Procopius had once described it, rose from the water in front of them like "an exhalation in the night". Unlike the Crusaders who accompanied him, the blind Doge was undaunted by the sight of the fourteen miles of land and sea walls that had previously repelled rapacious armies of Avars, Sasanids, Arabs, Bulgars, Russians, Attila "the scourge of God", and assorted Turkish tribes before him. The land walls having been enlarged to their final configuration in 413 by Theodosius II, the grandson of Theodosius the Great, were undoubtedly a marvel of military construction, arranged in a double row behind a wide moat, with a formidable no-man's land between them.[1] In addition to this lethal combination, nearly one hundred huge towers along the walls, placed at regular intervals, protected the main gates to the city that were placed between them, so that any invaders could be assaulted diagonally from above to best advantage. Each of the gates, in turn, were named according to either an identifying characteristic or the section the city that they gave access to, such as the White Gate, or the Gate of the Lifegiving Spring. While one of the Byzantine names for Constantinople itself may have been Theophylaktos, or "Protected of God", equal credit for the 1000 years of safety before the Venetian invasion should also be given to the man-made cliffs of brick and stone that combined with a naturally defensive topography to keep the city secure. The bronze equestrian quadriga that had crowned the main doorway of St Mark's Basilica in Venice (until it was removed recently to protect it from air pollution) had originally been brought from Rome by the Emperor Constantine as a centrepiece for the Hippodrome of the new city that was to bear his name. They were themselves based on a Greek work done in the second half of the 5th century BC, and were just a small fraction of the treasure that the Venetians carted out of the city after a desperate nine-month long struggle that had brought about its tragic destruction. It is sad to think that the richness of the Piazza San Marco, which has been so admired for centuries, was gained through the desecration of what had been the only existing repository of the classical traditions of Greece and Rome, and that this represents only a hint of the treasure that was taken.

Byzantium and the city that the Crusaders and Venetians of 1203–4 had looted, had its beginnings in the 7th century BC, when King Byzas from Megara in Greece, first saw it to be a uniquely defensible location on which to establish his small kingdom, surrounded as it was by the Marmara Sea on the south, the Golden Horn on the north and the swift deep waters of the Bosphorus at its tip. This wall of water on three of its sides made only subsidiary walls along the shore and a single land wall necessary in order to make any settlement there totally secure. A legend

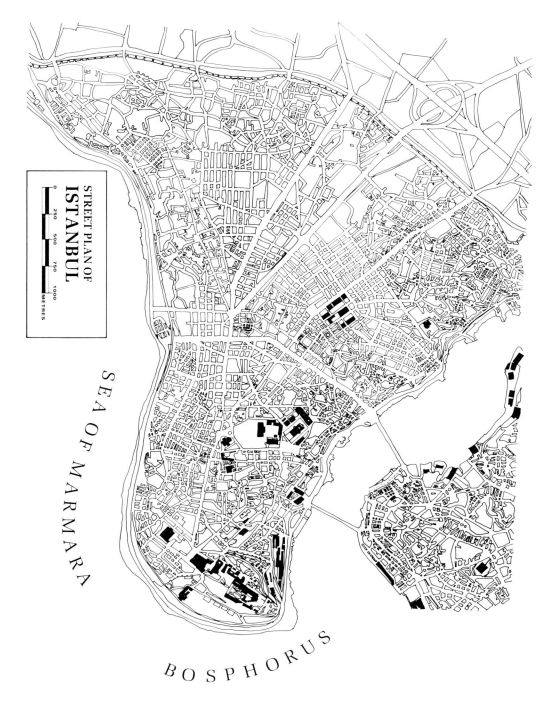

STREET PLAN OF
ISTANBUL

0
250
500
750
1000
METRES

SEA OF MARMARA

BOSPHORUS

Figure 1 The gridiron layout of Constantinople/Istanbul

surrounding Byzas' choice of this site for the new city relates that after he consulted the Oracle at Delphi, he was told to build opposite "the land of the blind", in clear reference to the lack of vision of the Greeks in Chalcedon, who failed to seize it first. Byzas established the first settlement at the tip of the peninsula at a place now called Sarayburnu, or "the Nose of the Palace", because a royal residence has been there ever since.

Because of its strategic location between the Hellenic West and the Persian East, with the power to control sea and land traffic between two continents, the new city quickly took on a key role in the Persian wars of the 5th century BC, as well as in the Peloponesian War between Athens and Sparta that followed. Byzas' city, which was then nearly 200 years old, suffered several invasions by each side in the later war, as each tried to gain the upper hand in the important political arena of Anatolia. It was eventually the Persians, who, by using their navy to help the Spartans, managed to turn the tide against the Athenians, leaving the city at rest. The whirlwind passage of Alexander the Great through Byzantium on his way into central Anatolia and beyond, at the beginning of the Hellenistic age, opened up a new chapter in the history of this entire area, of which few indications except fragments in the Istanbul Archaeological Museum now remain.

The Romans were not far behind Alexander with the establishment of the province of Asia in 133 BC, and their greatly expanded ambitions, matched with unparalleled engineering ability, had a much bigger impact on the city than anything before. After three hundred years of relative quiet during the Pax Romana, ill-conceived political alignments in a Roman factional struggle brought retribution by Septimus Severus in 196 AD, who levelled and burned nearly everything standing in the city. Following this conflagration a new wall was built that stretched from the entry of what is now the Galata Bridge across the peninsula to the Sea of Marmara, nearly doubling an urban area primarily restricted in the past to the Acropolis. The rapidly increasing inability of the Roman empire to defend and hold its far-flung frontiers against outside incursions as well as the agitation of a growing Christian population within it, led to a momentous change in the historical course of what had been, until then, a relative small city within its control. Having succeeded his father Constantius Chlorus as one of the tetrarchs in the tripartite system set up by the Emperor Diocletian, Constantine was not content to share power but methodically set out to eliminate the other members of the ruling faction. His final victory over his brother-in-law Licinius, ruler of the West, at Chrysopolis, now Üsküdar, in 324 AD left him as sole ruler of both the eastern and western factions of the Roman empire, clearing the way for his decision to move its capital and establish a New Rome at Byzantium.

This decision was not made lightly, but was the culmination of Constantine's long experience in this part of Asia Minor during the reign of Diocletian, when he had held a government post in Nicomedia and had seen an extensive building programme carried there.[2] Constantine's New Rome was intended not just to be a substitute for its famous Latin counterpart, but a superior mirror image. Where Rome had seven hills and fourteen regions, its new replacement was to have them as well, even if a seventh hill had to be partially built to keep the parallel. Constantinople was also not to be deficient in riches and glory, as thousands of pieces of sculpture and other works of art were imported and manufactured to adorn the new city, which used the Severan plan as its base.

This plan already included temples, a hippodrome, and the baths of Zeus-Xeuthippes, a hyphenated deity of Thracian and Anatolian origins, and all of these played a favourable note in Constantine's decision to move his capital here. His plan augmented the pre-existing Roman structures in several important ways which are instructive of his long range intentions for both the character of the new city and its role as the centre of his new empire. Constantine first altered the combination of temple, circus and bath that he had inherited from Septimus Severus by replacing the pagan religious building with a pair of Christian churches which he named Hagia Sophia (Holy Wisdom) and Hagia Eirene (Holy Peace) in order to subtly ease the transition from old customs to new. As Hanfmann has pointed out, figures representing the concepts of wisdom and peace had been used in Roman buildings like the Celsus Library in Ephesus, which pre-dated the naming of these two churches and thus would have sent out a crystal-clear message that Constantine intended this city to be the heart and conscience of a new Christian empire, just as Rome had been the epicentre of a pantheistic one. To extend the revision even further he linked his own palace directly to the twin churches, which along with an elongated hippodrome whose form can still be traced today, and set up what Constantine felt to be the utopian triumvirate of "palatium, sacerdotium and circus" or palace, church and stadium.[3] Virtually nothing of the great palace remains now , but it has been suggested that it was probably very similar to Diocletian's huge residence in Split, which was a city within a city.[4] By inserting the palace into the old reciprocal relationship between temple and circus (which had effectively replaced the theatre as an institution of social gathering and entertainment at this time), Constantine symbolically put himself in the position of arbiter between the church and the people. Considering himself to be a thirteenth apostle who was destined by God to expand the mission of Christianity on earth, he saw himself as the leader of both the Church and the State, without favouring one to the exclusion of the other.

From this metaphorical head, located at the peninsular tip of the city, a spine, or regia, ran through the old barrier of the Severan walls to an oval forum of a size and form similar to that found in Jordanian Jerash [Gerasa] today. Like the *cardo maximus* of that almost perfectly preserved Roman city, its sides were lined with columns with shops behind them, continuing a late Roman trend toward the extension of the commercial activity of the old Greek agora along the street itself. This oval forum, which was later transformed into the Forum Taurii during the reign of Theodosius I, was the first major processional event prior to the square Philadelphian Forum to the west, where the main cardo branched in two in order to conform to the widening of the peninsula at that point. The northerly branch of the two ran parallel to the Aqueduct of Valens, past the Constantinian Mausoleum and the Church of the Holy Apostles to the Charisian Gate in the land wall.

The second branch turned along the coast of the Sea of Marmara to the south, running through the Forum Bovis and the Forum Arcadii to the Golden Gate, which was the main entrance into the city from the land side. The Constantinian plan for New Rome was remarkable for both the speed with which it was implemented and its adaptation of what had become a standard gridiron formula onto a challenging, hilly topography (figure 1). It is important to note that Constantinople did not spring up *de novo*, but rather was an extension of both the early city plan of Byzas and the Severan rebuilding of that plan. As such, it re-used the main elements of the middle avenue or *mese*, the tetrastoon agora, which became known as the Augusteion under Constantine, the Zeus-Xeuthippes baths, and finally the major north-south orientation of the hippodrome which was greatly enlarged to fulfil a wider social function.[5] In spite of its Christian basis, the city was not, however, totally organised around religious foundations as was its Ottoman counterpart, but closely followed the template of its Roman model.

The subsequent long line of Byzantine emperors that followed Constantine in a continuous 1,200 year succession, that was broken only by the Venetian interregnum, considered itself to be the rightful heir to a classical tradition that had been saved from certain extinction after the fall of Rome. For them, the physical resemblance of their city, in its final form inside the Theodosian land walls (plate 1), was too close to that of its fallen parent on the Tiber to be mere coincidence, and was instead considered to be Divine Will. The gradual evaluation of that classical heritage, during a remarkably long period of political stability threatened only by internal theological debates, was characterised mainly by a constant embellishment of Constantine's original concept of the unified duality of Church and State. The emperor and the patriarch both continued to refine their roles based on the original idea of a delicate balance between the two.

The Hagia Sophia (plate 2) remains as the best formal expression of the wish to perpetuate a classical heritage in the Byzantine East, and to record the separate but equal status of the emperor and patriarch meeting beneath a great dome was meant to symbolise the witness of heaven above. Ranking as one of man's greatest architectural achievements the plan of the Hagia Sophia clearly expresses the blending of the classic Roman basilica with circular Byzantine dome fitted to a square base. Anthemieus of Tralles, who became the architect of record after the death of Isadorus of Miletus, was a past director of the Academy of Athens and a noted geometer in the best Platonic tradition, making him the perfect bridge between the traditions of ancient Greece and those of Byzantium. Transcending its role as a purely religious building, the Hagia Sophia has become one of those rare monuments that now represent an entire culture, not merely a single function. The domed typology of the Hagia Sophia, due to its great imperial symbolism, was thus eagerly adopted as a model for all future mosques in Istanbul, regardless of the purely canonical origin of its centralised form.

The Ottoman empire, which at its zenith almost encircled the Mediterranean Sea, encompassing the Tigris and Euphrates valley as well as Syria, the Balkans and Greece, ruled that world from the "Sublime Porte" of Istanbul for nearly 500 years. Each of the highly visible tops of its seven hills became a preferred building site for sultans or emirs who wished to build a mosque or charitable foundation, which led in turn to a radical alteration of the skyline of the Byzantine city. Research into the documents involved with the building of these monuments, however, shows that the only criteria used for site selection was the desire for clean air or a clearly visible elevation rather than any comprehensive plan for a unified, domed and spired silhouette running the entire length of the peninsula. The final result, then, while extremely impressive, is another of history's fortunate accidents, a series of events totally unrelated to uniform aesthetic concerns or a comprehensive urban strategy.

It is understandable that an event as cataclysmic as the Turkish conquest of the eastern capital of Christendom would bring about other major adjustments in both the form and population of the city, which took about a century to be fully realised. Since Constantinople's population had gradually but steadily diminished prior to the conquest, Mehmet II found himself the sovereign of a virtually empty city. After some tentative attempts at resettlement that were generally resisted because of the sultan's initial refusal to grant ownership of real estate, a dual policy of land grants to prominent citizens and *waqfs* (religious endowments), as well as forced deportation and resettlement, totally reorganised the existing urban fabric, giving it a new social mix. New districts, bearing the names of origin of people resettled from Karaman, Trebizond, Belgrade or elsewhere, began to spring up throughout Istanbul as people began to pour into the vacated city. Eventually this chaotic and somewhat haphazard policy of repopulation became more systematic, once the essential need for a basic citizenry had been satisfied. Certain classes or trades from various areas throughout the Ottoman empire also began to be relocated en masse specifically because they could be of some exact service to either the court or the city.[6] In addition to this influx of culturally diverse ethnic groups, Mehmet also drastically altered the Byzantine make-up of the city by introducing the Ottoman *külliye* into common use. Basically a self-contained village unto itself, the külliye is a complex providing social services symbiotically related to a mosque, providing housing facilities, kitchens, hospitals, schools and libraries which are meant solely for the welfare of the public. This new institutional type had within it the seeds of a totally distinct urban organisation, and it progressively transformed Istanbul into an Ottoman city. The imperial külliye gradually occupied the key points of the urban fabric and the city's continuously linear structure, which had been virtually fixed since the time of Theodosius, but was progressively replaced by a discontinuous, point-by-point configuration that has left an indelible mark upon it. This large scale system of monumental punctuation allows great readability of the urban area today.[7]

Between the time of Sultan Süleyman and the end of the 19th century, Istanbul's population nearly doubled, growing from 500,000 to 900,000. In that time the accumulation of külliye and new settlements had completely altered the main axis of the Byzantine city, which had primarily been parallel to the Marmara coast, to one along the Golden Horn which linked the Bayezit, Süleyman and Fatih complexes together. With the opening of the first Ottoman customs office between the Sultan Ahmet and Bayezit Square near the Golden Horn, a new urban focus began to be established, but the old city walls on the west restricted further development. Because of this restriction all new growth in the city extended along the Bosphorus, including Kadıköy and Üsküdar, which at first were totally separate settlements of unique character divided by wide fields and gardens. Professor Doğan Kuban has shown that fountains as the primary water source of the village and that a comfortable walking distance to each helped to determine boundaries.[8] He has also estimated that prior to the 16th century, 62.4 percent of all Istanbul's mosques were located in the old city with the remainder scattered among the Bosphorus settlements, while in the 18th century this ratio dropped to 45 percent on the peninsula and 55 percent outside.[9] All of the new settlements along the water's edge helped to establish the Bosphorus as a major water transport lane, gradually transforming the image of the entire region even further. Along with the new axis of development along the Golden Horn, additional spines were established from Sircige to the west and from the Old City across the Golden Horn to Taksim and Harbeye where a large influx of foreigners at the end of the 17th century established a vibrant colony that continued to grow there for nearly two centuries. The growth of this second axis corresponded to a general move toward Westernisation in Istanbul at this time. Called the "Age of the Tulips" because of all the new gardens that seemed to spring up overnight, it was a period characterised by a general liberalisation and social *joie de vivre*, as well as a growing governmental interest in cultural development. A series of military setbacks prompted several successive sultans, such as Abdülhamid I, Selim III and Mahmut II, to make a determined effort to re-organise the Ottoman army between 1774 and 1839, despite stubborn resistance from both the elite army core of Janissaries and the *ulema* (clerics). One important result of these reforms was the introduction of foreign military advisers and their dependants into the city and the creation of new military schools and barracks, built along Western lines, that became the focal point of expatriate compounds around them. These changes eventually led to a series of reforms or *Tanzimat*, enacted in 1827, which inevitably altered the predominantly oriental customs and manners of Istanbul. The wearing of turbans was officially banned in 1827, followed by the publication of the first newspaper in 1831, opening of a postal service in 1834 and the replacing of the title of Grand Vizier by that of Prime Minister in 1836. Slavery was outlawed in 1846, followed by the opening of universities, as well as schools of medicine and art. Between 1846 and 1868, Ottoman embassies were established in many foreign countries, which also gave Turkish students a chance to study outside the country. As a final important step, a Magna Carta was passed in 1856 that guaranteed the rights and equality of all of the people in the empire regardless of religion or ethnic background.[10]

As a result of the prevailing governmental attitude toward Tanzimat, and with the advent of the industrial age at the turn of the century, the pace of westernisation quickened. New railways were built that connected Istanbul to Europe as well as to other cities in Turkey, making it the hub of industry and trade, and had a significant impact on its economic structure. New banks, attracted by this change, flocked to the city to take advantage of its increased wealth. Steamship services started in 1850, with six ships, and eventually led to the building of the Hyderpasha Port in the same year, and the Galata Port in 1909, all of which were a great impetus to economic activity in Istanbul.

This new openness to Western technology and culture also led to the first of what were to become an ongoing series of city plans, that followed the lead of those then being implemented in the major cities of Europe. The first of these was prepared under the supervision of Marshal von Moltke, who, in imitation of Baron von Hausmann in Paris, proposed the opening of fourteen-metre wide boulevards and avenues through the traditionally closed and dense urban fabric of the city. Aside from improving transportation links between different parts of the city, one of the most important rationales for this approach, apart from its being in vogue at the time, was the wish to create broad vistas to highlight large monuments more effectively, by isolating them within wide open spaces. While the width of the avenues proposed by von Moltke was later reduced by half, the basic concept of the destruction of large sections of the traditional city fabric was firmly implanted and remained as a feature of all of the thirteen plans that were to follow. As Andre Barry has said: "The structure of Istanbul, rooted in Islamic tradition [saw] initial changes over the course of the 19th century. . . . This introduction to modernisation in an oriental city where life follows the rhythm of the call to prayer, where 30 percent of the buildings are devoted to religion, is going to progressively overturn the customs of a people inclined toward contemplation."[11] The ideas that were instituted by von Moltke and refined in the next plans by Alfred Agache in 1933 and Professor Martin Wagner in 1936 were finally crystalised in the famous Proust Plan of 1937, which continued to be implemented up through 1950.[12] Focusing again on methods of transportation rather than the traditional values of the people, the Proust Plan concentrated on establishing major highways on all three shores of the Istanbul peninsula, basically replacing the area previously taken up by the sea walls.

In addition, new cross axes were proposed at roughly the same places where the land walls of Septimus Severus, Constantine and Theodosius had been built, linking the Marmara Sea and the Golden Horn with wide belts of asphalt that cut through the old city. This plan has been incrementally implemented and has completely disrupted the existing urban texture; just as similar highways have destroyed the old city of Cairo, which had previously only been capable of coping with pedestrian scale movement. Proust, in his "Archaeological Park" idea, has left buildings like the Hagia Sophia and the Yeni Cami standing alone in the midst of vast open spaces, where in the past they had been an integral part of the urban context. Another far-reaching, and often misunderstood, impact of the Proust Plan was a basic underestimation of Istanbul's potential for continued capital growth following the shift of the centre of government to Ankara by Atatürk in 1923. By proposing the location of what he felt would only remain light industry along the Golden Horn, Proust virtually assured the destruction of much of its natural beauty as that industry inevitably grew.

All of the remaining urban plans commissioned since Proust, namely those of the Revision Committee in 1951, Musavirler Heyeti in 1956, Hans Hogg in 1960, Luigi Piccinato and Gecis Donemi Tedbirleri in 1961, the Bakanliklararasi Commission plan of 1966, the Greater Istanbul Plan of 1967 and finally the Metropolitan Plan of 1972–1981, were all ideologically based on the same philosophy of von Moltke and Proust, revolving around the creation of wider streets and a "social museum".[13]

When Atakurk made the momentous decision to move the capital of Turkey from Istanbul to Ankara for security reasons in 1923, Istanbul lost political dominance within the country virtually overnight, but began to find a new economic role for itself around 1950, which was a turning point for the modern city. In the first part of what has been called the Republican Period, from 1923 to 1950, Istanbul's loss of position as the political heart of Turkey brought about the loss of its social, economic and cultural lifeblood as well. The aristocratic and bureaucratic associations of court life that the city had enjoyed for so long diminished as quickly as the empire it had once ruled. Prestigious residential areas, such as those around Bayezit and the Sultan Ahmet Square which were just becoming fashionable among court officials at the time of the move, immediately lost value and were either demolished, or suffered the slow destruction of being let room by room. The beginning of rural migration which has so dramatically affected other countries such as Egypt in this century, also brought Anatolian farmers streaming into Istanbul at this time. This migration not only brought the city population above 1,000,000 for the first time in its history but also started a critical shift in its social balance, from a traditionally polyglot ethnic mix of Turks, Armenians, Greeks, Levantines, Jews and others, to a primarily rural Anatolian stock. Consequently, many minorities, who have historically formed the basis of a well-to-do bourgeoisie in Istanbul, and who also gave the city a high degree of social texture, now found themselves being pushed out, and started selling their property to avoid the human tidal wave moving in from the countryside. In a classic example of the unexpected repercussions of the rash use of technological development, this rural migration has been shown to have been ironically accelerated by the well-meaning intentions of the Marshall Plan, which introduced the first mechanized tractors into Anatolia after World War II. From a preliminary donation of 1,750 tractors in 1948, the numbers shipped to Turkey steadily increased to 6,500 in 1950, to 42,000 in 1960 and 100,000 in 1970 — all of which had the incremental effect of causing a redundancy in manpower, subsequent joblessness, and a mass flight to the city to find work along the greatly improved highways that eased the process.[14] The peasant saying that the roads of Istanbul are paved with gold, does not always prove to be the case, and adjustment can be difficult. In 1979, for example, a survey of the Süleymaniye area uncovered hundreds of itinerant workers living in one of the kiosks of the mosque complex, providing a specific example of the slow takeover of many parts of historical buildings, as well as a general profusion of *gecekondu*, or squatter settlements, around Istanbul.

Following its loss of social and economic status in the Republican Period, Istanbul entered a second phase of development after 1950. A switch to a multiparty system in the country at this time, and subsequently a more liberal attitude toward economic development has meant that Istanbul has not only regained its old momentum, but today stands as one of the most cosmopolitan cities in the world. As a result of what might be characterized as mural, dendritic growth, the rings of Istanbul's walls, like the rings of a tree, have radiated out, one after another, from the first wall around the base of the old acropolis. This growth, when overlaid with the overlapping changes of axis in the Byzantine and Ottoman cities and the contemporary legacy of Proust, have resulted in a city with totally separate, highly individual and identifiable zones. These zones, which give Istanbul a uniquely staccato character, are related in turn to the squares that have emerged from the archaeological park idea, usually, but not always, centred around an Ottoman külliye or mosque in their midst.

The Sultan Ahmet Square, which is the oldest of these and which also incidentally provides the closest fit to any preconceived notions that a visitor expecting to find the exotic splendours of the East in Istanbul may find, is totally dominated by the presence of the Hagia Sophia, which remains aloof as a perpetual symbol of the aspirations of two successive cultures. For nearly 800 years after it was first commissioned by the Emperor Justinian over a millennia ago, on the site of the original Constantinian church, it represented the largest covered space in the world, with a dome as high above the ground at its apex as the top of a modern fifteen storey skyscraper. Built in the remarkably short time of five years and ten months, it served as a church for the first nine centuries of its life, and then, after the fall of Constantinople, a mosque for five more until it was finally declared a national museum in 1935. The dome, which peaks at fifty six metres above the floor and has a total area of 18,000 square metres, has partially collapsed three times. The first of these happened only twenty years after construction due to the subsidence of the Devonian rock beneath a foundation struggling to deal with its great weight and the plastic flow of bricks and mortar unable to cope with the great speed of construction.

The heart of the structural concept of the Hagia Sophia is a central circular dome carried on four arches that spring from enormous piers laid out in a perfect square (30.97 metres to a side). Pendentives which were a crucial Byzantine addition to Roman architecture, and made possible the transition from a square to a round form for the first time, connect the corners of the square to the dome, at the arches. There are, in addition, large half domes that open up the east-west axis of the space, which are in turn supported on secondary piers and colonnades.

The Hagia Eirene (plate 3), which has always been the companion church of the Hagia Sophia, is frequently overlooked by those who are more interested in seeing its more famous sister. A great treasure in its own right, regardless of its small scale, the Hagia Eirene represents a visible synthesis of Graeco-Roman, Byzantine and Anatolian traditions. Used as the first church of the empire prior to the completion of the Hagia Sophia, the Hagia Eirene has been party to as much, if not more, historical intrigue as its more famous companion. The most significant feature of the interior of the building is the *bema*, or series of steps in the apse, which served as the seating area for the clergy and a distinct descendant of the magistrate's throne in the Roman basilica type which served as a model for the Christian church.

The Sultan Ahmet or "Blue" Mosque, which lies south-west of the Hagia Sophia and gives this square its name, is so called because of the beautiful tiles in its interior. Built under the patronage of the fourteenth sultan of the Ottoman empire, this mosque, which was designed by one Mehmet Ağa, was completed in seven years and opened to the public in 1616. Because of the difficulty in finding land of adequate size for the mosque, the units of its külliye were scattered randomly all around the northern edge of the Byzantine Hippodrome, which is also located here. Among these, one section of old *arata*, or shops, today serves as a mosaic museum, and another portion is now being restored in the hope of returning it to its original function. The other parts of the complex, such as the kitchen used to feed the poor, a mental asylum and a workshop for the manufacture of swords, are now located within the ground of the Economic School of Marmara University. The parts of the külliye that are best preserved are the mausoleum of Ahmet I and a *medrese* which is used today as a state archive.

The Sultan Ahmet Mosque in its primary location at the tip of the Istanbul promontory, is the first in the series of mosques that seem to follow in line down the length of the peninsula. Covering a built area of 64 x 72 metres, excluding its courtyard, the building is modelled after the Şehzade Mosque which was built by the great architect, Sinan, 68 years before. Following the pattern established by the Hagia Sophia, the main prayer space is covered by a dome that is 24 metres in diameter supported by four large round columns that stake out the corners of the square space below. This main dome is buttressed, in turn, by four semi-domes, which expand that space a great deal.

Due to several hundred windows that penetrate both the domes and the walls, the mosque is generally better illuminated than the structure by Sinan that it was patterned after, allowing the tiles in its interior, the masterwork of a craftsman named Çinici Hasan Usta, to be seen to best advantage. An interesting aside in the design of the building is that a reduction in the anthropomorphic method of measurement called the *zira*, which was used by the masons at this time, from 60 to 24 fingers in width, has resulted in a marked difference in the proportions of the mosque, making it quite unique among the others of the classical period.

Possibly the most famous building on the Sultan Ahmet Square, however, must be the Topkapı Palace which stands at the highest point of the tip of the peninsula, exactly where the ancient acropolis had been. After Sultan Mehmet II had conquered Constantinople in 1453, he first thought to build his palace in the Bayezit area because the Saray-i Atik, or Old Palace as it was called, was already there, having replaced Constantine's Great Palace as the residence of the Byzantine emperors after the 11th century. Not totally satisfied with this choice however, Mehmet decided to build at the Sarayburnu perhaps because of its almost mythical connections with the city's imperial past. After the Byzantines had abandoned it, a hospital and a home for the elderly had been built here in the 12th century, as well as several monasteries which stood on the Marmara side of the hill. Construction of a new palace, or Saray-i Cedid, was started in 1467 AD, on a slope overlooking the water which ensured a constant breeze and sweeping views of Galata, Üsküdar, Marmara and the juncture of the Golden Horn and Bosphorus below. Continuously altered during the following 400 years of its use, the palace constantly evolved into the eclectic complex seen today (figure 2, plate 4). In the course of that evolution an extension of one of the pavilions built over the sea walls took the name Topkapısı, or Gungate Pavilion, because of the cannons strung out along the shore below. With the building of the railroad in this area in 1863, this pavilion was removed, but the name remained and eventually replaced that of Saray-i Cedid for the whole complex. In 1478, Mehmet the Conqueror ordered the construction of the 3 metre thick Sur-i Sultan or Sultan's Wall around the palace, which joined with the old Byzantine walls to encircle the entire site.

Having more or less arrived at its general form by 1465, the palace complex progressively decreases in size and degree of public access in successive courts that are each surrounded by their own wall, and each entered by a grand gate. The first of these is the Bab-i Humayun or Imperial Gate which leads to the Alay Meydani or procession centre, the scene of countless opulent audiences and reviews of elite Janissary corps in the past. The Janissaries, whose name is a corruption of the Turkish phrase *Yeni-Ceri*, or "new force", were an elite army recruited to serve the sultan. The Alay Meydani was relatively accessible to the public during ceremonies, and was rimmed with utilitarian spaces such as bakeries, armouries, servants' residences and storage rooms which must have filled it with a buzz of activity.

One of the most beautiful buildings in the Alay Meydani, or First Court, is the Çinili Köşk, which is sometimes referred to as the Şişe Saray or Glass Palace in court documents of the past. Having been built in 1472, prior to the palace wall itself, the kiosk is set above a high platform which acts as its base, and is fronted by an impressive colonnade that precedes a centre court flanked by four iwans. The blue tiles that decorated this interior, which are flecked with gold and alternated with white, provide an unusual catalogue of faience styles from different regions of Turkey all brought together here. The Jerid field which once preceded the kiosk, now holds the Istanbul Museum of Archaeology, which is frequently overlooked, but holds great treasures. The transition from the First Court to the second is marked by the middle gate or Bâbüsselâm which is flanked by towers on each side and capped with turrets. A macabre attraction of this gate is the Cellâd Çeşmesi, or Executioner's Fountain, where he used to wash his axe after each execution. The

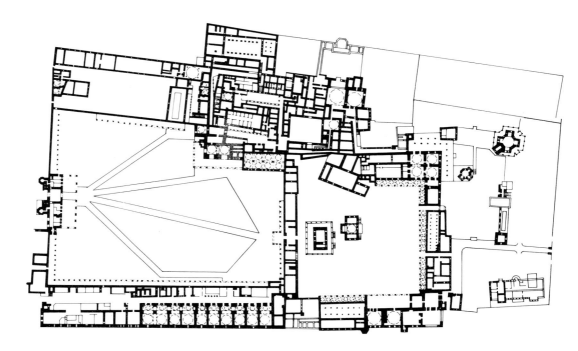

Figure 2 Topkapı Plan.

sultan alone was allowed to proceed past this gate on horseback to enter the divan court beyond, which was, in reality, a large garden surrounded by arcades and galleries. Written evidence in the palace library indicates that this court was heavily planted with large shady trees and laced with curving stone pathways that were then commonplace in Turkish landscape planning. Looking at the straight, flat concrete pedestrian expressways that have now been installed to handle the large crowds that visit the palace each year it is hard to imagine just how different this enclosure must have been.

The Divan, or Imperial Council, met in this court, as did the Janissaries, for ceremonies and financial allotments, in a monthly display calculated to impress all those present with the incredible wealth of the empire. Regiment by regiment, the troops would march past the reviewing stand of the sultan to receive their *ulufe*, or salary, in front of the seated ambassadors and foreign dignitaries invited to attend. Coronations or *culus*, would also take place here, reinforcing the ceremonial character of the space.

On the right hand side of the court, three gates gave access to the kitchens, as well as the housing of the staff that ran them. The kitchens themselves, whose domes and chimneys are an unmistakable part of the palace skyline, were built by the architect Sinan in the 16th century and are an organizational masterpiece, divided into units that were meant to serve separate groups of people reported to reach 10,000 or more on certain days. Today, the kitchens are quiet, only housing one of the world's most valuable collections of Chinese porcelain. At the far end of the court are the barracks of the Tasselled Halberdiers who were charged with taking care of the fires in the Harem. The tassels on their helmets, which gave them their name, were not only decorative, but were meant to prevent them from seeing the odalisques as they carried out their tasks.

As one of the oldest sections of the palace, the ward of the Tasselled Halberdiers is exquisitely decorated with floor and hearth tiles, lacquered flowers engraved in wood, and a technique of working in gold, called *edirnekari*, which is used on the windows. On the left side of this court, beside the imperial assembly which gives it its name, is the Carriage Gate or Araba Kapısı, which leads to the Harem and which is also the most popular part of the palace today. A square, 40 metre high tower, meant to be a watchtower for all of the palace grounds, marks the entrance to the legendary seraglio which is a maze of nearly 300 rooms, only a small portion of which are open to the public today. Containing not only the women's quarters, the Harem also housed the Black Eunuchs who guarded them, the sultan's private apartments and those of his family and relatives. Not originally a part of the palace complex, the Harem was built by Sultan Selim's son, Murad III, in 1574.[15]

A complete world unto itself, the Harem (plates 5, 6) was in reality not the scene of the hedonistic orgies it is often imagined to have been, but was instead the domain of the Valide Sultan, the sultan's mother, who had complete control over it, and only introduced the few select girls she found favourable to her son, using the Kahisa Kadin or Head Stewardess as her instrument. As may be imagined, such an arrangement led to a great deal of intrigue among the women there, who were chosen from all over the empire. Tales of bored women being placated by drugged sherbets, while true, are exaggerated. The Harem was instead a closely knit matriarchal society, into which the sultan could only intrude following carefully prescribed etiquette, on special silver shoes whose unmistakable clanking on hard tile floors would announce his presence. The Harem also effectively served as a gaol for relatives and offspring who were deemed to be a threat to the sultan, and even those young princes not thought to be so were confined there for schooling until they were quite far into manhood. Because the Harem as an institution was felt to have effectively isolated future leaders from both the outside world as well as the day-to-day decision-making of the court, it has been cited by historians as one of the prime causes for the weakening of the Ottoman empire in later years.

Basically, the Harem consisted of three main divisions, the first of which belonged to its guardians, the Black Eunuchs. The second belonged to the Valide Sultan and the Haseki Sultan, his primary wife, as well as ladies-in-waiting, concubines and servants. The third and last section was given over entirely to the sultan's private apartments. Directly after the Carriage Gate, which got its name because of the charmed few Harem residents who left there by carriage to go shopping in Istanbul, was the Nöbetyeri, where the Black Eunuchs stood guard over the main entrance. A small prayer hall, called the Black Eunuchs' mosque, stands close to the Nöbetyeri, as does their main court, which is accessible through a large metal gate and is among the most impressive spaces in the entire Topkapı Palace complex. The court is also surrounded by the chambers of the Hazinedar, or treasurer, and the Chief of the Black Eunuchs.

The Princes' School also located here deserves particular mention in that its extremely ornate, baroque revetments were designed in 1749 by Beşir Ağa, who was the Chief of the Black Eunuchs at the time and who was later executed in 1752, for unspecified reasons. The beauty of the decoration indicates that these men were more than just mindless guards, armed with huge curved scimitars, as they are so often portrayed. Beyond the courtyard of the Black Eunuchs is the Cariyeler, or inner court of the concubines, which gives access to their quarters above. These are far less extravagant than those of the Black Eunuchs, almost resembling a prison. Below the court is the concubines' hospital, whose size indicates that their life was less than idyllic. As further confirmation of this, a stairway running down from the hospital leads to a morgue in the basement whose only exit is the Meyit, or gate of the dead.

The Bab-i Sa'adet, or Gate of Felicity is the entrance to the third court of the Topkapı complex and is contemporary with its founding. The entrance itself is domed, and framed by extended arcades that give it a more delicate feeling than the Ortakapi that precedes it. The throne of the sultan was placed under the domed canopy of the gate on ceremonial occasions and it was here that he, as commander-in-chief of the army, would receive the holy banner of Islam before each military expedition. Also called the Akağalar, or the White Eunuchs' Gate after the troops that were used to guard it, it leads to the Enderun, and Arz Odasi, which is the throne room of the sultan where foreign ambassadors and dignitaries were both presented to, and took their leave of, him. Moving in from the Gate of Felicity on the left hand side of the Third Court, is the Kutsal Emanetler, or Treasury of the Sacred Relics, which is a square building divided into four sections each covered with a dome. Known to those inside the palace as the Hirkai Sa'adet, or Pavilion of the Holy Mantle, this section not only housed the garment it was named for, but other sacred relics of Islam specifically brought here from Egypt by Sultan Yavuz Selim, who was known in Europe as Selim the Grim. Carefully guarded, the Kutsal Emanetler was ceremoniously visited only on certain special holy days, when the sultan and his retinue would stay in the Arzhane, or Presentation Room and have the relics brought out to them. A number of the relics belonging to the Prophet Muhammad and the four caliphs that succeeded him still survive here, so that many people from all over the Islamic world come to visit this section of the palace. In keeping with the religious nature of this section of the palace, the Ağalar Mosque, as well as the Harem Mosque were also located here. The Ağalar Mosque, which was intended for those in the Enderun, (which was an important school for the higher education of Janissaries who showed great promise) has since been turned into a library for rare manuscripts and houses many exceptional and priceless miniatures. Hilary Sumner-Boyd, in describing the crucial role of the Enderun has said: "This elaborately organized school for the training of the Imperial Civil Service appears to be unique in the Islamic world . . . the pages who attended the school came from the Christian minorities of the Empire . . . and received a rigourous training, intellectual and physical, which in contrast to the usual Islamic education was largely secular and designed specifically to prepare the students for the administration of the Empire. There can be no doubt that the brilliant success of the Ottoman state in the earlier centuries was to a large extent due to the training its administrators received in this school.".[16]

Vaulted passageways at the rear of the Third Court lead into the fourth and final compartment of the carefully differentiated succession of spaces that make the Topkapı palace so unique. Where the Second and Third Court are enclosed, the Fourth Court is planned around the spectacular panoramic views of the Golden Horn far below. A series of kiosks are strategically placed on different levels across the narrow expanse of the terrace that both complement and contrast each other in form and personality, making this stepped garden a sculpture court of broad eaved pavilions. Perhaps the most famous of these is the Baghdad Köşk, which was built in 1639 in honour of the Ottoman conquest of that city in the same year. Attributed to the architect Kasim Ağa, this broad eaved kiosk rests on a high podium and is supported by many columns. Like the Revan Köşk, it has four iwans that radiate out from a domed central space, all of which are covered with the most beautiful tiles imaginable, and lit with coloured glass windows that create ever changing patterns on the walls and floor of the interior. The kiosk has been placed at the extreme right hand side of a paved area called the Marble Terrace, at the centre of which is a delicate canopied viewing pavilion called the Iftariye, or Feast of Ramadan Pavilion, because it has been used by sultans in the past to receive guests during the festivities associated with that period of the Islamic year. Built by Sultan Ibrahim in 1640 AD. the exquisitely worked and gilded roof, which is inscribed with verses related to him, is supported by extremely thin columns, allowing an open view of the Incirlik, or Fig Park immediately beneath it, and the city far beyond. Acting as a hub for the other pavilions on the terrace that wheel out from it, the Revan Köşk, also called the Sarik, or turban room in the past, was built by Murad IV to celebrate the capture of Erivan in the expedition against Persia in 1635. The Revan Köşk is rather small in scale, and is faced inside and out with exquisite tiles that line the curved interior face of its central dome and the ceilings of its four iwans as well. The kiosk is historically significant as the scene of a bloody massacre in 1730, when Sultan Mahmud I lured Patrona Halil and his followers there on the pretext of conferring the title of Grand Vizier upon the revolutionary leader. When they arrived, they were all killed by the sultan's huge bodyguard, Pehlivan Halil Ağa, (who was also a famous wrestler of the time), in revenge for the overthrow of Sultan Ahmed III, and the assassination of his own Grand Vizier, Nevşehirli Ibrahim Paşa, two months earlier. The basement of the kiosk, which is always cool because of its massively thick stone walls, was also used for the preparation of the bodies of dead sultans, adding to the dark shadow that the slaughter of Patrona and his group has cast on its beauty.

A wide, shaded arcade separates the Revan Köşk from the Pavilion of the Holy Mantle behind it, linking it with the Sunnet Odasi, or Circumcision Room, a single space used for the ceremonies marking the entry of a young prince into manhood.

The Iznik tiles, which are remarkable throughout the palace, are outstanding here. On the Marmara side of the Fourth Court a sense of enclosure is achieved by a linear complex of buildings, the first of which is called the Esvabi Odasi, or the Room of the Robe, followed by the Sofa Mosque, which was built in 1859, along with the Yeni Köşk, which is next to it. The Mecidiye Köşk, which effectively turns this line of buildings, creates an enclosure called the Lala, or Sultan's Tutor garden. In a slight play on words, this name was later changed to the Lale, or tulip garden, in recognition of the flower that was to become an obsession in Istanbul in the beginning of the 18th century. In contrast to other famous Islamic gardens, such as the Alhambra in Granada, or the Royal Meydan in Isfahan, Iran, the Topkapı Palace is unusual because of the progressive unity of its spaces. In the Alhambra for example, each open space and the accompanying buildings that surround it, are conceived as separate and distinct units which are aesthetically self-contained, having little or no visual or physical connection with those adjoining them. In the Topkapı, however, the spaces, which are also interiorised and compartmentalized, are sequentially linked in scale, proportion and overall character, based on the desired degree of public or private access to them. An oriental philosophy, similar to that found in the Forbidden City of Peking, and which seems to indicate the common ethnic root of both designs, judges the royal procession from exterior to interior to be the unifying link in the spatial chain of spaces, rather than the highly individualised character of each.

A fitting finale to a visit to the Topkapı Palace is a stop at the Konyali Cafe which is on the opposite side of the Treasury, in the Third Court. Arranged on several tiers that each give an unobstructed view to the water below, the cafe offers an excellent selection of Turkish food at its best.

Recently, Çelik Gülersoy has initiated several extensive restoration projects throughout Istanbul. One of the best of these is the Ayasofia Pansiyonlari, which is a row of 19th century wooden townhouses attached to the wall that separates the grounds of the Topkapı Palace from the open square around the Hagia Sophia. Now reorganised as a hotel, the Pansiyon, while a bit contrived, offers a good place from which to experience the special character of Sultan Ahmet Square. Because of the townhouse format, the scale of the hotel is intimate and residential, with the rooms on the opposite side of the wall, overlooking a narrow cobblestoned alley, giving wonderful views of the Hagia Sophia directly across the way. The Sarnıç Restaurant, which is also a Gülersoy project, terminates one end of the row, and is a converted Byzantine cistern. While both the cuisine and accoutrements are slightly regrettable, the space itself is much more impressive than its original function might suggest, and the restoration has been very well handled. In addition to the Sarnıç, the Pansiyon has also converted one of the houses in its midst into a restaurant for the use of its guests. Several other hotels, such as the Konak or Yeşil Ev, which are also close to the Hagia Sofia, are also projects that Çelik Gülersoy has converted using the same basic approach as in the Pansiyon.

The Sokullu Mehmet Mosque, which is a small treasure of Islamic architecture created by the architect Sinan in 1572, is located on the southern side of the peninsula at the far extreme of the Sarayburnu, near the end of the hippodrome. Named after a famous grand vizier in the count of Süleyman the Magnificent, the complex was actually commissioned by the vizier's wife, Esmehan, who also happened to be the daughter of the sultan, Selim II. Originally consisting of *medreses* (religious schools), baths, shops and a caravanserai, which have not survived, the complex was skillfully organised on a sloping site, which the great architect Sinan turned from a liability into an asset at the main entrance (figure 3). As one approaches a small square in front of the entry gate, stairs are seen to lead up under the massive wall facing it into a courtyard in front of the mosque itself. By going up those stairs, the ablution fountain in the middle of the court, as well as the arcade surrounding it, and the main elevation of the mosque, slowly emerge into view (plate 7).

The marble paved courtyard is surrounded by a portico of pointed arches, behind which are *medrese* classrooms that were used for religious education. The interior of the building is dominated by a large dome, the drum of which is supported by arches resting on two buttresses that spring from the entrance, as well as from each of the sidewalls. The lateral areas are covered with small semi-domes which peak at the bottom level of the drum. A major feature of this mosque is its extremely fine, long and narrow *mihrab* (niche), which is built of Marmara marble, and the crown of which is gilded. The *minber* (equivalent to a pulpit), which surrounds it, is widely recognized as one of the finest masterpieces of tile workmanship in Istanbul, incorporating calligraphy into the composition in a very integral way. Sinan, more than any other architect, has normally shown a preference for verticality in his medium-sized mosques, but here it is an essential complement to the magnificent Iznik tiles which are used, so that space and ornamentation work together as one. Professor Doğan Kuban has described this mosque, as "an impeccably unified space where the plan, elevation and domed roofing constitute a totally integrated whole."[17]

No visit to Sultan Ahmet Square, or to its extension in Kadırga, where the Sokullu Mosque is located, would be complete without a stop at St. Sergius and Bacchus, which is close by. Representing a vital step in the marriage between the

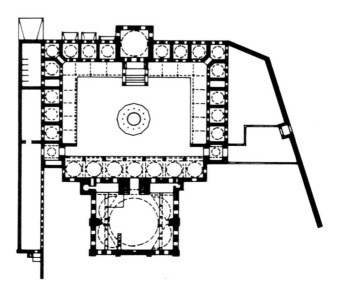

Figure 3 Sokullu Mehmet Pasha, plan.

centralized martyria and the linear basilica which was realized during the highly experimental architectural period of Justinian's reign, this church had a critical impact on the design of the Hagia Sophia which followed it, and therefore upon Byzantine and Turkish religious architecture as a whole.

After Sultan Ahmet, the next major square in the old part of the city is Bayezit, which is also known as Hürriyet Meydani, connected to the Sultan Ahmet by the Divan Yolu and the Yeniçeriler Caddesi, or Street of the Janissaries. As is often the case in this city, this square takes its name from the mosque complex in its midst, which here is the oldest one still intact in Istanbul (plates 8, 9). Having been built in 1505, by an architect named Hayrettin Ağa, the mosque fixes, once and for all, many of the canons of classical Ottoman architecture, standing as a final synthesis of several parallel traditions. The mosque of Bayezit acts as an important transition point for many disparate buildings around it, close to one of the main gates of the Grand Bazaar, or Kapalı Çarşı, the Sahaflar Çarşısı, where rare and new books are sold, and Istanbul University, which has stood on this spot since the conquest in 1453 (figure 4).

The Kapalı Çarşi is the commercial counterpart of royal Topkapı, a city within a city, consisting of nearly 3,500 shops under one roof. In addition to the shops, there are mosques, restaurants, workshops, schools and fountains within that combine to give this bazaar a scope and variety that easily make it one of the most interesting markets in the Middle East. In this labyrinth of shops, each trade has traditionally been allocated its own place, creating special streets for goldsmiths, carpet sellers, and so on. Because of the relative narrowness of the passageways, the dim light, the overwhelming number of shops and the incessant sales pitches of one merchant after another, the bazaar can be an unnerving experience for the uninitiated. A clear idea of the general categories of things available in it, is usually a good idea, always allowing for the chance discoveries that make this market such an adventure. A carpet, or kilim, is almost a must, having long been a symbol of Turkish craftsmanship. Choice, however, can be a problem, as the sheer number and attractiveness of the samples offered make one seem as desirable as the next. If a knotted carpet seems expensive, the flat woven *kilims*, or *cicims*, with their strikingly unique Anatolian designs and bright vegetable dye colours are always a possibility, as are goat-hair rugs. Other than carpets, the best items to be found here are hand painted ceramic plates from Kütahya, handmade copper and brass trays and cauldrons, embroidered *heybe* bags, *yastik* cushions, hand embroidered *oya* lace, locally made meerschaum stoneware and pipes, gold jewellery and leather. Also, for the more serious collector, the old, or antique, Bedesten which was originally put in the centre of the bazaar for security reasons is, as it has been described "a place of safety where funds could be deposited and where all sorts of financial transactions took place . . . [It] played the role of semi-official banking house. With the perfect regularity of its architecture it constitutes a landmark in the trading quarter in contrast with the relatively indecisive geometries of the shops that have accumulated around it".[18] Care should be taken, however, in buying anything considered to be antique in Turkey, as strict laws preventing the exportation of national treasures have recently been enacted, and many fakes are now also being produced. Protracted and patient bargaining, over several cups of tea or Turkish coffee also seems to be a prerequisite, in direct proportion to the cost

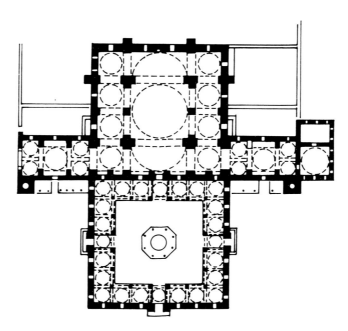

Figure 4 Bayezit Mosque, plan.

of the object in question, and serious purchases should not be rushed.

The Mahmut Paşa Yokusu, which is one of the exits of the Kapali Çarşi, on the opposite side of Bayezit square, leads past the old Sandal Bedestan, or Silk Bazaar to the Mahmut Paşa Mosque (figure 5). This mosque, which was built by the grand vizier to Mehmet II in 1463, originally contained 265 shops of its own, although none of these now survive. At first glance the mosque recalls the reverse T-plans of the Bursa period, but close examination reveals several important modifications. The plan shows a very creative approach to the resolution of the common problem of keeping the interior segregated from the main entrance. In the centre of the building two axially placed domes, which are eleven and a half metres in diameter, cover the prayer space below by means of a broad arch which links the two and is a unique feature in this mosque. Doors on each side of the main prayer area open onto side corridors which are covered by vaults, and iwans opening off each of these, add to the compositional individuality of the plan organisation. These side spaces, as is the case in other reverse T-plan mosques, can either be used for social activities, or as *medrese* classrooms, giving the impression that the designer simply took the traditional *medrese* plan of the past, of a courtyard and three iwans, and incorporated it into a mosque plan in the search for a combined unit. The porch of this mosque has suffered major alterations as a result of repairs conducted in the 19th century, and fires in the covered bazaar nearby have also affected a great many parts of the building, requiring further work.

In direct contrast to the inventive approach taken with a traditional plan in the Mahmut Paşa mosque, the Nurosmaniye or "Light of Osman" Mosque near it (plate

10), which was built 300 years later by Sultan Osman III, displays a deliberate preference for Western, and specifically Baroque European, models. As Professor Doğan Kuban has described it: "With its elliptical courtyard, exterior articulation, its huge cornices and its dependent buildings organised around courtyards [it] is one of the most attractive buildings in Istanbul."[19]

Bayezit Square, with its frenetic and closely packed mixture of commercial, educational and religious institutions, is far different in character from the stately and spacious vistas of Sultan Ahmet, where the full effects of Proust's idea of a "historical park" can be most readily visualised. Bayezit, in turn, is also more intimate in feeling and far more scaled down than Süleymaniye, which is next in the sequence of major urban spaces in old Istanbul. As is the case with those that have preceded it, the focal point of this area is the religious complex of Süleyman

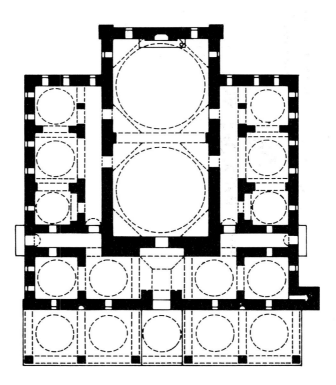

Figure 5 Mahmut Paşa Mosque, plan.

the Magnificent, also known as Kanuni, the Lawgiver, the longest reigning sultan in Turkish history. Having extended the Ottoman empire to the apogee of its power between the years 1520 and 1566, he is also remembered for the racial and religious unanimity that characterised his reign. Sultan Süleyman, who made a habit of personally leading his army in battle, died in a military encampment in Hungary, and was buried in a mausoleum in the courtyard of this mosque which bears his name (plate 11).

Sinan the Great, who was the architect of the complex, was almost fifty years old when he was given the title of Chief Imperial Architect, and lived to be nearly one hundred. In the course of that long career, he also became an authority on public works, and the professional guild system, and organised architects, carpenters and masons into cohesive groups. He was also known to be a disciplined, non-stop worker. Born of Christian parents in Karamania in 1490, Sinan is known to have been trained in the elite Ottoman Janissary Corps, and to have seen action in many military campaigns throughout Europe and Asia, where he learned mathematics, geometry and acoustics in the design and construction of many military buildings. After leaving the military, he is also known to have worked on nearly four hundred different projects, including many throughout the empire. Many of the young people involved in this organisation also later went on to become famous architects in their own right.

The Süleymaniye Mosque and the complex surrounding it, which is one of the most famous of Sinan's buildings, was built in 1557. In addition to the mosque, the Külliye consists of four *medreses*, a Koranic school, an elementary school, a medical school, a hospital, a public kitchen, a hospice, a post graduate school, a bath, and mausolea, with the various parts surrounding its vast inner courtyard seeming to slowly build toward the hemispherical volume of the mosque's dome. The harmony achieved in the massing of all of these different types of buildings is extraordinary, especially when seen over the tops of the low buildings in the streets nearby. After entering the central courtyard and noticing that it opens up toward a vista of the Golden Horn and Bosphorus at its eastern end it becomes obvious that Sinan deliberately built the *medreses* to frame the view in that direction.

In the Şehzade Mosque, Sinan had previously created a wide, central space, using four hall domes to support a large dome in their midst. Yet, in the interior of the Süleymaniye Mosque he rejects a similar approach, which would have yielded a larger volume, in favour of two half domes, which reduce the prominence of the main dome and improve the overall incremental massing. In addition, the side aisles are covered with three successive domes, with the one in the middle raised higher than the other two in order to link these aisles to the scale of the central space. The marble columns supporting the roofs of the side aisles follow this overall desire for volumetric unity by being so lean that they are hardly noticed, and do not appear as dividing elements. Although the plan is not symmetrical, the interior space builds up uniformly, successfully and sympathetically uniting a monumental building complex with the much smaller scale urban context that surrounds it.

Without getting involved in a discussion of Sinan's use of proportion and numerical harmony, it should be noted that he also indulged in some symbolism here as well, using four minarets to denote Süleyman's position as the fourth Sultan after the conquest of Constantinople and ten balconies on the minarets to signify his being the tenth Ottoman Sultan since Orhan-Bey.

The construction of the Süleyman complex was undertaken with Sinan's usual organisational abilities, which were abetted in this particular instance by the full mobilization of the army to help with both the construction and the supply of materials, shipped to Istanbul from the farthest extremes of the empire. Although interior ornamentation in the mosque was kept to a minimum, a well-known calligrapher named Kul Hasan Çelebi of Karahisar contributed greatly in this area, to the extent that he went blind in the process. Sinan, in writing to a friend about his work on the project wrote that: "after Kanuni called me, I went straight to the Palace, where I was asked how long the building would take. I told him right there and then that it would be finished within two months. Work continued day and night and one day the Sultan came to me and asked me if I would be able to keep to my word. I told him yes. At the end of the two month deadline, the building was finished, and I passed the key over to the Sultan's blessed hands; after which I folded my own in prayer. The Sultan, on turning to his own representative who was present, asked whom he felt most deserved to open the mosque. He replied by saying 'My Sultan, your most humble servant Sinan, the Master Architect, is a saintly old man, and therefore I feel that this honour belongs to him, as he is one of your most devoted subjects.' After the Sultan had heard these words, he willingly handed me the key, with praise, saying: "It is most fitting that you open this house of God.' Uttering a prayer, I opened it."[20] The modest mausoleum of Sinan is still located in the northern corner of the outer courtyard, reflecting the humility that made him the greatest Turkish architect of all. The district of the Süleymaniye, perhaps more than any other in the city, shows the extent to which the Ottoman institution of the Külliye completely revised the urban tissue of Istanbul. The Şehzade complex nearly, which may for all intents and purposes be considered a part of this section of the city, reiterates this very theme, even if on a much smaller scale (figure 6).

Moving north from the Süleymaniye complex, the Şehzadahası Caddesi, which eventually turns into the Fevzi Paşa Caddesi, runs past another major complex dedicated to Fatih the Conqueror, on the left. Begun ten years after the capture of Constantinople, and completed in 1470, this mosque, which was commissioned by Mehmet II, was built over the Byzantine Church of the Holy Apostles, and the monastery that supported it (figure 7, plate 12). When the mosque and its subsidiary structures, which are just as numerous as those of the Süleymaniye, were greatly damaged by an earthquake in 1766, Mustafa III, who was the sultan at the time, ordered that extensive repairs be carried out between 1767 and 1771, resulting in an almost total rebuilding of the mosque. Only the walls of the inner courtyard in addition to the ablution fountain, the main doorway and some parts of the main walls of the mosque have remained (plate 14). A centralised dome plan has been used in the reconstruction of the mosque, freely borrowing from the plans of other mosques such as the Şehzade, Sultan Ahmet and Yeni Cami. In this application, the central dome rests on four piers, surrounded by four semi-domes; and the overall feeling of the building, rather than following the Baroque style that was in fashion during the time of the rebuilding, respects the original concept in every way possible. The mausoleum of Mehmet the Conqueror, the scourge of the Byzantines, is located behind the *qibla* wall (indicating the direction of prayer) of the mosque, and was a special focus of attention in 1952, on the occasion of the 500th anniversary of the Ottoman capture of the city, when the entire complex was repaired once again.

Before circling around to Eminönü and crossing the Galata Bridge over the Golden Horn, it should be noted that by continuing to follow Fevzi Paşa Caddesi to the old Theodosian land walls, through the Edirne Capi or Edirne Gate, the street

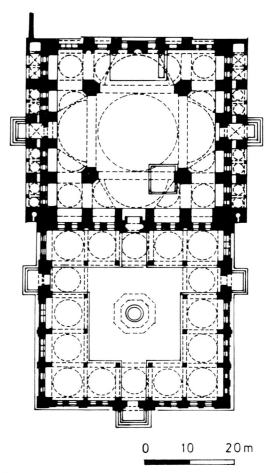

Figure 6 Şehzade Mosque, plan.

will eventually lead to Eyüp, a village now a suburb in the north of Istanbul, on the shore of the Haliç. The Mihrimah Cami, near the well-known Kahriye Cami at Edirne Kapı, is another of Sinan's masterpieces, built between 1550 and 1555 on the orders of Süleyman the Magnificent's daughter, Mihrimah Sultan, the richest woman in the world at that time.[21] This mosque may be considered one of the most interesting of the medium sized buildings built by Sinan due to the complex aesthetic impact he is able to achieve with very simple means. As is often the case in the rare instances when an architect is able to do this, it is hardly possible to imagine how the structure of the building could have been solved in any other way. In the front of the mosque, there is a large courtyard surrounded by a portico that must have preceded a *medrese* on each side which have now gone. In the interior, piers standing in each corner of the main square prayer area that support the dome above, give the illusion of being partially inside and partially outside the interior space, since finials are used to counter the weight of the buttresses as they often are

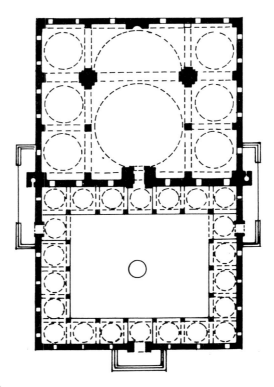

Figure 7 Fatih Cami, plan.

in Gothic cathedrals. On the exterior, the piers, capped by the finials, emerge through the wall, and end just at the springing of the dome. The window-wall of the mihrab is the most memorable part of the mosque, with a seemingly infinite number of colours having been used to make up each of the openings. This use of colour in the windows, combined with the green, red and blue tile work throughout, creates an unforgettable impression.

The village of Eyüp, which is further on, is best known as the location of the mausoleum of Eyüp Ansari, who was one of the Companions of the Prophet Mohammed, and who served as a standard bearer under the command of Yezid in 671, during the Arab attack and siege of Constantinople at that time. Having been killed in the battle, he was buried in a mausoleum here which has given the town its name and has made the area a place of interest for Muslims visitors from all over the Islamic world. After the Ottoman conquest of the city in 1452, a scholar named Semsetin found a gravestone at the edge of a forest near the Golden Horn with an inscription indicating that it belonged to Eba Eyüp. On the orders of Mehmet II, a mausoleum was built over it, and a mosque followed in 1458. This mosque has since been altered many times, the last overseen by Hussein Effendi, a vizier of Sultan Selim III in 1798. To the exclusion of several other mosques in the vicinity of the Eyüp Cami, mention should be made of the Zal Mahmut Paşa Cami nearby, which is considered to be one of Sinan's finest small-scale mosques. The complex, which also includes two *medreses*, a public fountain, and the mausoleum of its namesake, was commissioned in 1555 by Zal Mahmut, who was the husband of another daughter of Süleyman the Magnificent, named Şahsultan. The mosque, which is most interesting because of the way in which Sinan has resolved the expression of interior functions on the exterior facade, also shows clever handling of the use of levels imposed by a hilly site. From the higher level there is an entry into a court surrounded on three sides with a U-shaped *medrese* unit, which is linked by a stair to a second lower courtyard. This court served as a public fountain and rest area for travellers in the past, and also enclosed the mausoleum (figure 8). On the whole, the mosque looks quite compact, and the main dome is used to great effect as a central focal point (plate 13). The level changes made necessary by a difficult site have brought about some inevitable shifting of window locations from one side of the mosque to the other, which has all been handled very ingeniously. The walls of the building are laid with alternating courses of cut-stone and brick in a style that is reminiscent of the brick and rubble method used by Byzantine architects, particularly in Constantinople, the Aegean coast , and the Balkan territories, making it what Cyril Mango has called "the central tradition of Byzantine architecture".[22]

Eminönü, which is the last square that will be considered in the old city, is really an extension of the Bedesten which begins at Bayezit and works its way down the hill to the Golden Horn and the Galata Bridge below. The area, like its neighbour on the crest of the hill behind it, is a fascinating combination of elements in one place, such as the Spice Bazaar, or Mısır Çarşısı and the Yeni and Rüstem Paşa Camis which front the entrance to the Galata Bridge (plate 15). Unlike the Bayezit, Süleymaniye and Fatih areas, which are dominated by a main mosque and Külliye, the main visual impression of Eminönü is the noise and confusion of both the land and sea traffic at the water's edge, since this is a meeting point for roads going to other parts of the city and ferries travelling out into the Golden Horn, Bosphorus and Marmara Sea.

The Mısır Çarşısı or Egyptian Bazaar, is not as well known as its more famous counterpart, the Covered Bazaar, nearby and might easily be missed in all the visual chaos here were it not connected to the Yeni Cami. This connection is more than mere chance as the Mısır Çarşısı was originally intended to serve as a source of revenue for the perpetuation of the mosque in the past. A street has now partially come between the two, nearly breaking this link. The Yeni, or "new", Mosque is anything but, having been built in 1598 by Safiye Sultan, the mother of Mehmet III. Safiye Sultan was a rather interesting character in her own right, having come from the Bafo family of Venice. Her father was the governor of Corfu and during one of her trips between Venice and Corfu she was captured by the Turks. Because of her high rank and great beauty she was presented to Sultan Murad III, who married her. Her son Mehmet III eventually became sultan himself in 1595, making her the Valide Sultan. For various reasons it took 63 years to finally complete the construction of the Yeni Mosque, partially due to several architects having been dismissed for incompetence, as well as new turns in the saga of Safiye, who was put under house arrest in the Old Palace following the death of Mehmet III in 1603. In 1660, after opinions against her had changed, the construction of the mosque was begun once again under the patronage of Turhan Sultan, the mother of Murad IV. In

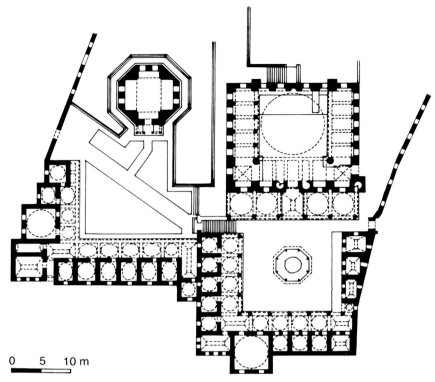

0   5   10 m

Figure 8 Zal Mahmut Paşa Mosque, plan.

order to provide a site that was large enough for the mosque, the houses of many Jewish families in this area had to be demolished, and they were re-settled in new villages along the coast of the Golden Horn.

The Rüstem Paşa Mosque nearby may be smaller in scale than its more visually dominant neighbour, but is even more architecturally significant because of the ingenuity that Sinan used in designing it. Having been commissioned by Süleyman the Magnificent's son-in-law, Rüstem Paşa, in 1661, the mosque is built in a market area filled with shops and warehouses. In order to separate the building from the din around it, Sinan has raised it up on a platform which not only insulates the prayer area from the noise of the bazaar, but also makes the mosque look larger than all of the other two-storey buildings around it (figure 9). Because of the restrictions of this platform, the building does not have the classical type of courtyard, but instead has stairs leading up to the entry from each of the two front corners which reach a long open terrace preceding a double portico. The first of these is low with a wooden roof, and the second is higher with domes covering it. A large dome is also used to roof the mosque interior, and is framed by lower side areas which are covered with vaults. As was usually his habit, Sinan has also built galleries over the lateral areas here, thereby providing the interior with an expansive spatial effect. One of the most important features of the mosque is the Iznik tiles which cover both the interior and exterior walls, since the period of production of the most beautiful tiles in Iznik coincides with the construction of the mosque. These tiles begin at the springing of the arches, and are used in calligraphic motifs as well. Unfortunately, much of the beautiful calligraphic work was later covered over by decorative elements in a pseudo-Baroque style.

The ferries that leave from Eminönü open a new world of exploration, as they travel up the Golden Horn and Bosphorus and out on the Sea of Marmara from this area, to go from Sirkeci to Üsküdar, on the Asian side of the Bosphorus, which was known as Chrysopolis, or "the city of gold" in classical times. This area is architecturally rich today because it was favoured by the Ottoman Valide Sultans as a location for commemorative works and was then much more quiet and rural than Istanbul itself.[23] The Yeni Valide Cami Complex, which is perhaps the most prominent, was put up between 1708 and 1710 by Sultan Ahmet lll's mother, Gülnus Emetullah Sultan (figure 10). The rather long courtyard wall of the mosque, which today only faces the parking lot used by cars at the ferry, has always been a prominent visual feature greeting visitors to Üsküdar. This wall shields an unusual ablution fountain in the centre of the courtyard within, which is octagonal in plan and covered with a dome carried on arches supported by eight round columns. All of the columns of the courtyard itself are sheathed in marble, creating a magnificent entry into the mosque. The interior organization of the building is very similar to that of the Rüstem Paşa Mosque, in Eminönü, with the exception of twenty-eight windows encircling the drum of the dome, which fill the interior with natural light. In spite of the fact that it was built in the early years of the "Age of the Tulips", this mosque does not blindly copy Western models, but reflects all of the characteristic features of the classical Ottoman style, providing a welcome reminder of a time when Istanbul and Üsküdar were both more tranquil.

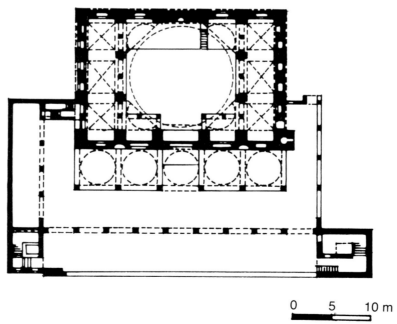

0   5   10 m

Figure 9 Rüstem Paşa Mosque, plan.

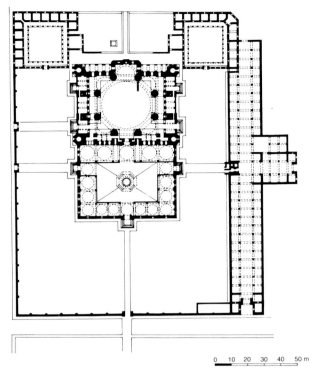

0 10 20 30 40 50 m

Figure 10 Yeni Mosque, plan

The Rum Mehmet Paşa mosque which is located on a slope to the south of the Yeni Valide Cami is an important inclusion in the itinerary of anyone visiting Üsküdar. It is evidently one of the oldest mosques in the city based on its Bursa-style plan arrangement. However, instead of using two domes as the Bursa mosques do, a semi-dome is used over the mihrab area, altering the standard formula used at the beginning of Ottoman architectural development (figure 11).

In plan, the mosque shows lateral areas that are also not the usual iwans seen elsewhere, but rooms with doors. The building underwent serious repairs in the fifties which resulted in most of the windows that allowed so much light into the interior having been closed. Yet in spite of the darkness, it is still possible to appreciate that the mosque presents a unique variation on a standard theme.

Four other mosques which also deserve mention in Üsküdar are those of Şemsi Ahmet, Mihrimah Sultan, Atik Valide and Ayazma Cami which are all relatively near the Yeni Valide and Rüstem Paşa Camis. The Şemsi Ahmet Paşa was built in 1580 by Sinan on a narrow road that is now cut off by the Üsküdar wharf, with the mausoleum of its namesake located between the mosque and the shoreline. A *medrese* stands to the west of the main building, wrapping its string of rooms around it like a protective shell. Both the *medrese* and the mosque share a common courtyard. Sinan achieves a very sensitive integration between the building and a waterside site here, showing that it is often possible to do much with limited means and area. The Mihrimah Sultan Mosque, which is also by Sinan, was built in memory of a daughter of Süleyman the Magnificent who later married Rüstem Paşa. Having been completed in 1547, it was originally very close to the shore of the Bosphorus, but is now about fifty metres away due to the development of this area. The mosque does not have the usual classical type of courtyard, possibly because Sinan thought that this would distort the harmony of the building's silhouette and its reflection in the water. Instead, he has enlarged the interior space of the building, and has projected it towards the sea. The Atik Valide Mosque, in contrast, cannot be seen from either the Golden Horn or Galata, as it is high on the hillside, shielded by trees. Among the last of Sinan's works, the mosque complex also consists of three *medreses*, a hospice, a clinic for the mentally ill, a bath and a caravanserai, which indicates that the complex served an important role as a terminus for the caravan roads leading from Asia. This would also explain the location of the complex near the old city gate, which would have prevented the caravans from entering the city itself. The mosque, at the centre of the complex is surrounded by a high wall, and the courtyard is rimmed with a deep portico. At the rear of the courtyard, *medrese* classrooms extend out towards the street, achieving continuation with it. From the structural standpoint, this mosque is considered to be one of Sinan's' most original works, with its large dome resting on six supports. Two of these are used to accentuate the mosque entrance, while the other four frame the mihrab niche and the side walls, respectively. The cemetery here contains gravestones which have great artistic value, and passing from the cemetery to the

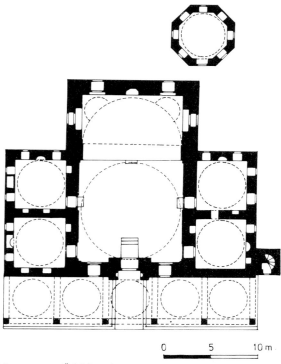

0   5   10 m

Figure 11 Rum Mehmet Paşa mosque, Üsküdar, plan.

first courtyard, a high wall separates it from a house, called a *mesruta ev*, that was built for the religious officers of the mosque, and is now evocatively surrounded by tall cypress trees. The Ayazma Cami, which is the last of this group of four mosques, is completely different from the others in style, having been built in 1760 by Sultan Mustafa III. A single compact mass is here offset by a delicate projecting portico, adorned with a large semi-circular staircase.

From Üsküdar, it is just a short ride by ferry or taxi to Anadoluhisari, passing through small villages and old wooden houses on the way (plate 16). This village, which was named for the towers in its midst, is dominated by their presence. Built as the Asian counterpart of the Rumeli Hisari or European towers across the Bosphorus, they were built very quickly by Mehmet the Conqueror to blockade the Bosphorus, and to prevent help and supplies from reaching Constantinople in 1453 (plate 17).

The village still has many good examples of the traditional wooden Turkish house that were very common in Istanbul, but have now become the victims of modernization (plate 18). The origins of this house type have been traced back to the yurt, or round tent that was used by the nomadic tribes on migrations into Anatolia, prior to urbanization, and has expressed itself in many different regional styles and materials. The most important factor in the transition of the shelter from tent to house was the family unit and its size. One of the changes inherent in adapting from a nomadic to urban lifestyle were the new domestic functions that agriculture demanded, and with them, the need to have larger families in order to keep up with the increased work required. Simple functions that were only designated to an area in the nomadic past were now becoming more complex and organized and were allocated to an entire room. Each of these rooms which was designed as an independent unit, was then grouped around a common ante-chamber and opened into it to allow full communication between all the members of the family. The eldest male member of the family, upon whom the welfare of all the others depended, held the highest position in its hierarchy, and so the male quarters logically assumed great importance in the design of the house. This room, called the *başoda* or *selamlik*, was a reception area used for the entertainment of male visitors only. As the next important member of the family, the wife typically spent much of her time indoors, and the design of the harem, or women's quarters, and interior courtyard reflected this need for privacy. Rooms related to the domestic activities associated with the wife, such as the dining area, were also located in the harem area.

There is no discernible difference in the size of any of these separate rooms and functional requirements do not seem to have had a significant impact upon their dimensions. The entry, called a *seki-alti*, or *pahucluk*, is always set one step lower than the rest of the house for sanitary reasons, and shoes were usually left there.

The *seki-üstu*, or living area, is lined with built-in divans running along the entire length of the walls, interrupted only by the fireplace, which is usually located across from the entrance. The hearth of the fireplace is flanked by niches, used to hold candles, lamps and domestic items, which were usually built at the same time as the house, and therefore integral with it. These were used to store the mattresses and pillows used for sleeping, so that the space itself was kept clear during the day. One of these closets was also used as a bath, or *gusulhane*, so that

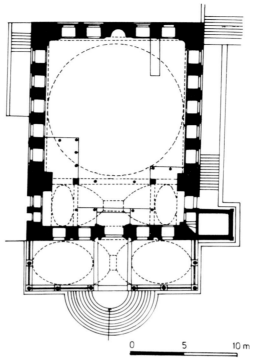

0   5   10 m

Figure 12 Ayazma Mosque, Üsküdar, plan.

it, too, was not visible until it was used. Usually two rows of windows separated by a shelf called a *yemislik* ran around the entire perimeter of the house. The top row was fixed, and let light into the space through highly decorative, tinted glass panes. The bottom row opened to let in air and was shielded by wooden screens for privacy.

As Doğan Kuban has described the house, "Women participated in street life only by watching it; the role of the woman must be properly stressed in the shaping of the house, and indirectly, in the shaping of the city. When the man returned from the outside world, he entered into this microcosm. The door opened onto the garden or courtyard set with trees, shrubs, small flowerbeds, and a small fountain or well. It was a self-sufficient world for the daily life of an average family . . . To explain the design of the house as being determined by the role of the woman is no exaggeration, for it is clear that, in the long run, the social as well as the economic status of women and the characteristics of the Islamic family have been decisive."[24]

As new bridges are constantly put up across the Bosphorus to ease the increasing traffic headed for Istanbul's growing suburbs, the areas demolished to make way for their bases threaten to eliminate even more of these traditional houses (plate 19).

The Beylerbey Palace, which is on the way to Anadoluhisari at the base of the Bosphorus Bridge, represents the opposite extreme of the vernacular tradition. Built by Nikogas Balyan, who was one of the famous dynasty of Armenian architects who succeeded by satisfying a growing royal taste for European architecture in the middle of the 19th century, it was commissioned by Sultan Abdül Aziz in 1865. A persistent, although unconfirmed story surrounding the palace is that it was really built in preparation for a visit to Istanbul by the Empress Eugenie with whom Abdül Aziz was infatuated, and whom he wanted to impress. The Beylerbey Mosque nearby, in spite of its baroque style, is not contemporary with the palace but was built by Sultan Abdül Hamit I in 1778. Unlike the classical relationship of a mosque to the other institutions in its Külliye which has been seen throughout other areas of Istanbul, the other sections of the institution are not connected to the mosque in this case, but for some inexplicable reason are located near the Yeni Cami in Eminönü (figure 13).

Another excursion by ferry from Sirkegi is along the European side of the Bosphorus to the landing at Beşiktaş. The whole area is dominated by the long, linear elevation of the Dolmabahçe Palace, another Balyan creation that was built for Sultan Abdül Mecit. This rather than the Beylerbey really represents the first true defection from time-honoured royal residence at the Topkapı Palace, which had been the home of every sultan since Fatih the Conqueror until this time. Costing the present day equivalent of about eighty million dollars and taking twelve years to build, (between 1844 and 1856) the Dolmabahçe Palace is a enduring symbol of both the strong desire for reform at this time and the level of extravagance which, as in Egypt, eventually lead to bankruptcy and the virtual mortgaging of the Ottoman empire to foreign powers in 1881 (plate 20). The Dolmabahçe continued to be used as a royal residence up to and through the reforms instituted by Atatürk in 1922, with the exception of Sultan Hamit II, who built his own palace at Yildiz

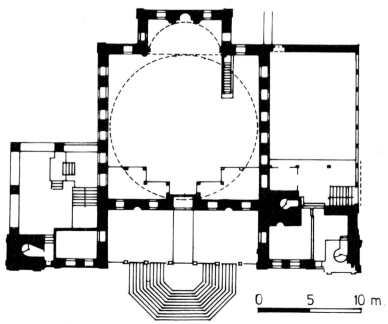

Figure 13 Beylerbey Mosque, plan.

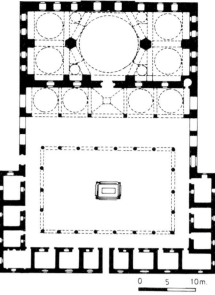

Figure 14 Sinan Paşa Mosque, plan.

in the park of the same name (plate 21). This palace, which was designed by an Italian architect named Raimondo d'Aronco, broke the Balyan monopoly on royal commissions and introduced the art nouveau style into Istanbul. It was followed by many other works executed between 1893 and 1909. After meeting Olbrich in Paris 1900, d'Aronco attempted to cross-breed the Viennese succession style with Ottoman forms, with mixed success. Works such as his Hyder Paşa army medical school, Karaköy Mosque, (now demolished), the Botter house at Istiklâl, the Mamdoh Paşa Library at Arnavutköy, and Cemil-Beyhouse at Kireçburnu, however, pale in comparison to his Şeyh Zafir tomb in Yildiz, built in 1983. This, as well as the summer house built for the Italian Ambassador at Tarabya in 1905 are almost surreal, and show the full extent of Olbrich's influence upon this gifted architect.

The Sinan Paşa mosque, which is directly across from the Beşiktaş ferry landing near the Dolmabahçe Palace, is another of master Sinan's works, built in 1553. Located symbolically close to the tomb of Barbarossa, who was probably the most well known Turkish admiral of all, the mosque is most significant for its re-interpretation of the Üç Şerefli Cami in Edirne, which in itself represented a dramatic step forward in mosque design. The Üç Şerefli Cami is undeniably seminal in the historical progress of Ottoman architecture and so its restatement here, in the hands of an architect as perceptive as Sinan, has an added importance (figure 14).

In this refined reading, however, Sinan expands the mosque forecourt in order to visually set off the large dome that he uses to best advantage, and surrounds that court with dependencies that are built into the enclosure wall rather than using the domed potential of the model used, and develops it to best advantage.

Further along the corniche which runs beside the Bosphorus, the Nusretiye

Cami, which follows its stylistic predecessor, the Nurosmaniye, by nearly seventy years, is an experiment of an entirely different sort (plate 22). Built by Kirkor Balyan, who was the patriarch of the family that irrevocably altered the skyline of Istanbul, the Nusretiye faces the corniche with a palatial two-storey facade rather than the classical courtyard of the Sinan Paşa mosque nearby.

A third excursion from Eminönü that should be considered is a trip to the Princes' Islands which are accessible from there, or from the ports of Kadıköy or Bostanci on the Asian side. These nine islands, which supposedly take their name from the Byzantine princes that either used them to escape the pressures of Constantinople or were banished to them, lie just far enough out in the Marmara Sea to seem very remote and isolated, and yet are just a short bracing boat-ride away. The islands, which each have delightfully prosaic names and vary in size, group around Büyükada, or Prinkipo as it is sometimes called, which is the largest. Walking past the restaurants and clubs that are clustered along the ferry slip and up the gentle slope toward the elegant wooden Victorian-style villas at the crest, the quiet narrow streets and absence of cars convey an impression of how Istanbul must have looked only a century ago. The Hotel Splendide here, which is one of a group of excellent hotels serving what has now become a very popular summer resort, contributes to this image of a by-gone era, with its delicate white gingerbread woodwork shining in the crisp light that seems unique to these islands.

The one final expedition from Eminönü that should be mentioned is a trip in the other Caddesi to the Piyale Paşa Cami, overlooking the Halic below (plate 23). Built in 1577 by the famous Ottoman Grand Admiral Piyale Paşa, the mosque is unusual in style, with an elongated main space covered by six domes making it very different in concept to other mosques of the classical period. Because Sinan was known to have been the major architect at this time, and as it is hardly conceivable that an admiral of Piyale Paşa's stature would have turned to anyone else for the design, the highly unconventional approach of the building makes it a controversial point (figure 15).

Galata, which is directly across the bridge of the same name from Eminönü, has a history that is intriguingly parallel to its more prominent partner across the Horn. Galata really came into prominence in 1261, however, when the Byzantine emperor Michael Palaeologus made a pact with Genoese merchants who wanted to settle there, in order to break the fifty-seven-year-long Venetian stranglehold over Constantinople

This first settlement, which was restricted to the shoreline, gradually expanded upward towards the top of the hill where the Tower of Christ, or the Galata Tower, now stands. From the very beginning, Galata represented an ethnic anomaly that stood aloof as the Turks encircled, sacked and burned Constantinople.

Their neutrality gained them relative autonomy under Ottoman rule, and as Muslim Istanbul grew, Galata remained, as it has been described, not only "a city within a city", but also "a western city within an oriental one."[25] As such, it attracted a mixed population of Levantines, Armenians, Greeks and Jews, who along with the Genoese formed a vital and convenient link to the west for the Ottoman empire. The Galata Tower, which is the major land mark of the neighbourhood today, has stood here since medieval times, having been built in 1348 as part of the expanding defensive system of this section of the city. Today it

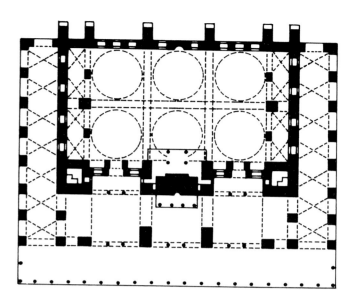

Figure 15 Piyale Paşa Mosque, plan.

is capped with a rather tawdry restaurant which caters mainly to tourist groups, but the view towards the old city from the balcony, especially seen at night when all of the major monuments are lit up, is unforgettable.

Beyoğlu, which runs north from the Galata Tower, along the ridge of a hill, means "lord's son" and refers to Alvisi Gritti, the son of Venetian Doge Andrea Gritti, who was a royal favourite in the 16th century Ottoman court and had an estate here.[26] Istiklâl Caddesi, or Independence Street, which runs through its midst, and which was opened by Sultan Abdül Hamid II in 1880, naturally became a magnet for foreign banks and embassies attracted by the unique status of the area. Also known as Grand Rue de Pera, this was the fashionable place to be seen. As Andre Barry has said, "The placing in service of the Edirne-Constantinople line allowed a direct connection to be established with Europe and it was not long before Pera became part of the legend. This was the era of the Orient Express, the Pera Palas and the Tokatlian Hotel, of La Marquise chocolates [and] Russian princesses in exile."[27] That elegant ambience, which has long since disappeared, has left several poignant reminders of the way things must have been. The Pera Palas Hotel still exists, looking much as it always has, in the days when Atatürk himself used to stay here. The management of the hotel, however, in realizing, as the restorers of the Orient Express have, that people will pay much to relive the past, have adjusted their prices accordingly. There is a story that many wealthy Russian emigrés, having left fortunes behind when escaping the Revolution, turned to jobs as food-and-wine tasters in the restaurants of Beyoğlu, because they had no other marketable skills. Rejans, which is another pocket of nostalgia here, seems like the kind of place that would have hired one. This restaurant, which is a shadow of its former self, lives on in faded grandeur, still serving Russian specialities such as beef stroganoff, saslik, and tavuk kievsky to those who can negotiate the winding alleyway that leads to it. Primarily a shopping street today, Istiklal Caddesi is still home to many banks and also has many side streets that are full of surprises. One of these, called Dudu Odlar Sokak, near Galata – Saray Square in the heart of Beyoğlu, is a maze of fishmongers stalls, flower shops and delicatessens such as Sutte, which is undoubtedly one of the finest in Istanbul. Other side streets in Beyoğlu are equally as colourful, perpetuating the free-wheeling reputation that Pera has always had.

Eventually Istiklâl Caddesi reaches Taksim Square, the contemporary equivalent of Sultan Ahmet Square in the old city, where Istanbul seems to come full circle from the past into the present. Here the redundant embassies of Beyoğlu, whose staffs have all now been transformed to Ankara where power is now, are gradually replaced by modern steel and glass hotels and office towers like the Etap, Sheraton and Hilton, that have all gravitated toward the nerve centre of this multi-faceted city. Named after a water distribution point that was built here in 1732 by Sultan Mahmut I, Taksim today might easily be mistaken for the centre of any major urban area in the world, a vast and frantically busy open space, choked with traffic all day long.

The hotel compounds here offer the only semblance of peace and quiet in this area, especially evident in the green space surrounding the Sheraton and Hilton Hotels. These parks, in turn, are linked by a bridge crossing over the busy intersection of Cumhurriyet and Yeni Dolmabahçe streets and are a delight in such a busy urban area. Neighbourhoods like Maçka, with chic shops and expensive townhouses vying with each other to corner the best views of the water, continue to surface, both here and on the Asian side, showing that this city is not just a prisoner of the past, but is alive and well. In Istanbul, at least, this past is like a fine, interconnecting web that has been intricately woven over the course of thirty centuries. Most of the strands, regardless of the incursions of time, are still visible, making this city a rarity in a world where entire sections of the past have been obliterated.

Prior to the capture of Constantinople in 1453, the Ottomans had systematically eliminated all the other Turkish principalities which had been competing for power in Anatolia, and had first established their capital in the Byzantine city of Brussa, taken after a ten year siege in 1326. Transliterated to Bursa by the Ottomans, this city, which lies at the foot of 2,543 metre high Ulu Dağ Mountain at some distance inland from the Marmara Sea, became an architectural testing ground for a fledgling state seeking visible legitimacy in its claim for expanding power. Using devices absorbed in aesthetic osmosis from the Seljuks, who had in turn expanded on the architectural advances of other principalities such as the Karahanids and Ghaznavids, the Ottomans continued to explore the effectiveness of large portals, processional courtyards, central axis symmetry with flanking iwans and intricate masonry techniques. Combining these elements with the dome, which the Byzantines had perfected and which was now subsumed as a symbol of the continuity of classical Western tradition in their hands, the Ottomans began to develop an entirely new monumental architecture here. As Walter Denny has described it: "form rather than decoration ... constitutes the main visual determinant of Ottoman architecture. Parallel to this, by the thirties of the 16th century, Ottoman architecture had evolved into a great number of well established genres quite unlike one another in form, although sharing common principles of construction and a common vocabulary of structural units . . . to a great extent the sources of these conceptions . . . are found in the genesis of Ottoman buildings themselves, Ottoman builders exploited the colours and natural textures of stone and lead, brick and tile, to an extent not reached by any other Islamic architecture in the 16th century."[28]

This genesis is palpable in Bursa in buildings like the Ulu Cami, Orhan Gazi and Yildirim Mosques, as well as in the famous Green Mosque and mausoleum complex (plate 24).

After Osman, who was the founder of the Osmanli, or Ottoman dynasty, there were five sultans in succession, namely, Orhan, Murad I, Yildirim, Mehmed I and Murad II, prior to the reign of Mehmet II, the Conqueror of Constantinople. The Muradiye Complex takes its name from the fifth sultan in this line, who established a burial ground for the royal Ottoman house here fourteen years before his own death in 1451. There are twelve graves here, encased in stone and covered with a thin layer of symbolic earth that is constantly planted with flowers. The inscription on Murad's own grave proclaims him as "Captain of the Warriors and Champion of the Holy War", yet he was haunted by the premature death of his four sons who preceded him here. The tomb complex is peaceful now, surrounded by trees and lush gardens (plate 25, 26).

In addition to being a treasure house of early Ottoman monuments, Bursa is also historically important as a silk weaving centre which grew with Ottoman power, continuing a tradition of silk weaving prevalent here since Roman times. Many travelogues from the 15th century comment on both the quantity and quality of the

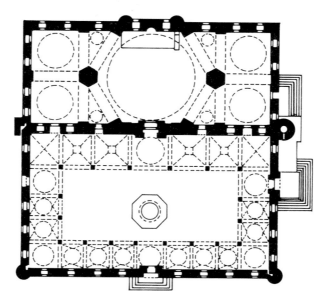

Figure 16 Üç Şerefli Cami, Edirne, plan.

silk trade in Bursa, comparing the results with the high level achieved in Damascus itself. Since Bursa was also the major centre for the European trade in raw silk from Iran, historians have determined that this fact alone may have served as a crucial factor in the formation of Ottoman foreign policy in the East, so that the trade might be retained.[29] The vogue for rich brocade fabrics among royalty in both Europe and Turkey, reflected in the textile collections of many museums throughout the world today, ensured Bursa's continued prosperity until tastes changed with the coming of the Industrial Revolution in the late 18th and early 19th century. From over 1000 looms in 1850, Bursa's manufacturing capacity was cut in half by the turn of the century when a growing preference for cheaper woollens and cottons made silk obsolete.[30]

Not content to rest on the record of such a rich history, Bursa today is undergoing something of a renaissance as a recreation centre, taking advantage of the slopes of Ulu Dağ as a ski resort in the winter and the thermal springs and cool climate at its base in the summer, which will undoubtedly ensure its continued prosperity.

Edirne, which was the second Ottoman capital, shares Bursa's architectural, if not environmental, wealth. Buildings such as the Üç Şerefli Cami, built by Murad II in 1437, and the Selimiye Mosque, which is Sinan's finest work, both bring the Ottoman saga full circle here, in one of the major cities of the Marmara region (figure 16, plate 27).

Notes

  1 Sumner-Boyd, H., *Strolling through Istanbul*, London, 1987, p. 370.
  2 Hanfmann, G. M., *From Croesus to Constantine*, Ann Arbor, 1975, p. 79.
  3 Ibid., p. 80.
  4 Mango, Cyril, *Byzantine Architecture*, Electa, 1978, p. 28.
  5 Hanfmann, G. M., op. cit., p. 86.
  6 Borie, Alain, et al., 'Istanbul', *Bulletin d'Informations Architecturales*, Institut Français d'Architecture, Singapore, 26 Dec. 1987.
  7 Ibid., p. 7.
  8 'Istanbul: Doğasi-Tariki-Ekonomisi-Kültürü', *Yurt Ansiklopedisi*, Istanbul, 1966, p. 6.
  9 Ibid., p. 7.
 10 Borie, Alain, et al., op. cit., p. 16.
 11 Barey, Andre, 'Along the Banks of the Bosphorus', *Lotus International*, no. 26, Milan, 1980, p. 21.
 12 Ibid., p. 23.
 13 Borie, Alain, et al., op. cit., p. 21.
 14 'Istanbul: Doğasu-Tariki-Eknonomisi-Kültürü', op. cit., p. 8.
 15 Sumner-Boyd, H., op. cit., p. 88.
 16 Ibid., p. 81.
 17 Kuban, Doğan 'Turkish Culture and the Arts', Istanbul, 1988, p. 25.
 18 Borie, Alain, et al., op. cit., p. 9.
 19 Kuban, Doğan, op. cit., p. 16.
 20 Goodwin, Godfrey, *A History of Ottoman Architecture*, London, 1971, p. 117.
 21 Sumner-Boyd, op. cit., p. 394.
 22 Mango, Cyril, op. cit., p. 9.
 23 Sumner-Boyd, op. cit., p. 420.
 24 Kuban, Doğan, op. cit., p. 32.
 25 Barey, Andre, op. cit., p. 23.
 26 Borie, Alain, et al., op. cit., p. 14.
 27 Barey, Andre, op. cit., p. 24.
 28 Denny, Walter B., 'A Sixteenth Century Architectural Plan of Istanbul', *Ars Orientalis*, vol. VIII, 1970, p. 55.
 29 Kuban, Doğan, op. cit., p. 104.
 30 Ibid., p. 105.

CHAPTER II
THE AEGEAN COAST

The Aegean coast, in its entire extent from Çanakkale in the north to Bodrum in the south, represents an unparalleled example of the historical layering that is so characteristic of Turkey in general and which has prompted the Ministry of Tourism to label this area an "open museum". As a mirror image of the Greek coastline on its opposite hand, this is the other side of what Socrates called the Hellenic "frog pond", and it is no surprise that the remnants of the classical age of Greece and Rome are most in evidence here. The destruction of Troy, which is where an exploration of what many Turks call the "Olive Coast" may most logically begin, not only marked the end of the Bronze Age, but also began a *symokismos* or repeopling of this part of Anatolia by refugees from that war. The premier city of the Troad, and the inspiring setting of Homer's *Iliad* was totally lost until Heinrich Schliemann made his famous, if brutal, excavations there over a century ago. Since that time, archaeologists using more sophisticated techniques have uncovered nine different levels of this city, and so far there is still no consensus as to which of these is the real city of the *Iliad*. Several historians, such as Ekrem Akurgal, use detailed analysis of each level to make a good case for a strata prosaically named VI-H, and for the destruction of the city by an earthquake rather than by Greeks concealed inside a wooden horse. Others vote for VII-A as the city of Priam, based on scorch marks on stones and other clues. Whichever of these actually is the Troy of legend is less important than the power of Homer's image, which has been strong enough to inspire so many in spite of the less than impressive state of the site today.[1]

Travelling to Troy from Istanbul by car presents two possible options that each have much to recommend them. The first of these is a car ferry from Sirkeci across the Sea of Marmara to Bandırma. From here there is a good road south to Lake Manyas and the national park located on its north east corner. Called Kuscenneti, or Bird Paradise, this park is known to have been set aside as a wildlife reserve since the Persian occupation of Asia Minor. From there it is a short way to Gonan, and then onto Dimetokda, near Granicus, where Alexander crossed into Asia in 334 BC to avenge Persian atrocities and singlehandedly began the Hellenistic Age. His first act on Asian soil was to pay homage to the Achaean cause at Troy, and to claim the shield and armour of Achilles whom he believed, with some justification, to be a distant relative. From Granicus, roads sweep south to Alexandria Troas, or west along the Dardanelles to the plains of Hisarlik, where Troy is located. The second option is to take the car ferry from Çanakkale which, while less romantic, is far more direct.

The city of Neandria, which is located at the crest of Mt Cigri about thirteen kilometres inland from Alexander Troas on the southern route from Granicus, has ruins that make those at Troy look extensive, and yet they are no less important for their scarcity. Recently discovered at the turn of the century by Robert Koldewey, this city, which was founded in the 5th century BC, covered a large area and was a thriving urban centre until the founding of Alexandria Troas a century later. The main importance of the site is that it is one of the first instances of the use of the Aeolic order, which took its name from Aeolis, the name of the district then and the Aeolian Greeks who settled here in the 10th century BC when trying to escape the Dorian invasion.

This style, which uses swirling, wave-like curves in its capitals, was very influential in the evolution of the Ionic order that followed and capitals in this early style that have been taken from the site can now be seen in the Istanbul Museum.[2]

Assos, which lies directly south of Troy, in the heart of what had been ancient Lydia, is one of the most interesting and little known cities on this coast. Now called Behramkale, the town is at the end of a small road that branches off the main road from Ayvalik and heads directly for the coast. Thought to have been built by colonists from Lesbos in the 10th century BC, Assos was one of the most important cities in the Troad prior to its capture by the Persians in 540 BC. Soon afterwards, between 348 and 345 BC, a local governor named Hermias, who had studied under Plato, founded a school of philosophy here, which attracted scholars such as Aristotle, among others, to the city. Eventually, Assos came under the suzerainty of the Attalid kings of Pergamon after Alexander's death and eventually was occupied by the Romans when the kingdom of Pergamon was bequeathed to them. Under Roman rule it was, of all things, best known for the sarcophagi that were made there and shipped all over the Roman empire. After the establishment of a New Rome by Constantine, Assos became a cathedral city of the Byzantine bishops, and was renamed Makramion after the Byzantine commander there. Due to visits by both St Paul and St Luke on their journey from Alexandria to Lesbos, and residence there by St Ignatius for many years, its early reputation as a stronghold of Christianity steadily grew. Although the port is the most active part of the town today, the most important part of the city in the past was the acropolis, 235 metres above it. The city was encircled and strongly fortified with entry gates and several of these, which are in a very good state of preservation, can still be seen on the acropolis today. A necropolis, used in both the Greek and Roman periods can also still be found near these gates. The agora, which is normally drawn in the textbooks as if it were laid out on flat land, was located half way between the acropolis and the port on a terrace carved into the hillside. Organized around an open central area that narrows toward its eastern end, the agora is ringed by multi-storey stoa that were lower on the downhill side to the north than they were on the south, allowing more light and better views to people walking through them. The temple of Athena, located on the centre of the acropolis, is rather diminutive, and is the only Doric temple in predominantly Ionic Asia Minor. The reasons for the choice of both scale and order here are interesting, and very informative of Greek sensitivity toward the close relationship between a building and the landscape. Vincent Scully speculates that a larger temple, in a more detailed order, would have been far too overpowering when seen from the bottom of the steep hillside, since the principal view to it was from the port there. In matters of aesthetics, then, Greek sensibilities would seem to have been guided by visual concerns rather than iron-clad tradition, allowing a variance here from regional custom.[3]

Around the gulf of Edremit, the village of Ayvalik has recently experienced a great deal of attention as a tourist destination because of its beautiful beaches, many new hotels and its proximity to Izmir airport. The view from Şeytan Sofrasi, or the flat "Devil's Table" hilltop to the Aegean below can be an unforgettable experience, as can the incomparable seafood served on Alibey Island just across the bay from the centre of the town.

Ayvalik can also serve as a good base for a trip to Pergamon, which is nearby. To fully understand the importance of this unique Hellenistic city, it is necessary to recall the chaotic situation in Asia Minor following Alexander's death when those closest to him lost no time in staking out individual claims to various pieces of the unified world he had dreamed of, and four main spheres of influence slowly began to emerge from the mêlée that followed his departure from the scene.

The most stable of these was Egypt, which was claimed by Ptolemy, one of Alexander's most able generals, as well as a prolific, if somewhat biased biographer of Alexander's exploits. In addition to territory within the official boundaries of Egypt as they are known today, Ptolemy also initially laid claim to most of what is now Libya, as well as parts of southern Syria and the Mediterranean coast of Asia Minor. The dynasty he began in 311 BC remained intact until Cleopatra backed the wrong side in a Roman civil war nearly 300 years later and it was ended by the battle of Actium. As a consequence of this relatively long and stable rule, thousands of Macedonians and Greeks settled in Egypt, primarily on land grants that were distributed under marital law.[4] As a result of this massive influx of foreigners, the richness of Egypt's ancient traditions was irrevocably altered and the culture changed to adapt to a new mix of people.

At a peace conference held five years after Alexander's death, Seleucus, who was the distinguished leader of his Shield Bearers, was recognized by the other successors present as the master of the old Persian satrapies of Asia, largely due to his capture of the city of Babylon nearly a decade after Alexander had died there. While the exact outline of the Selucid empire continued to ebb and flow thereafter, present-day Syria remained firmly in the midst of it. The Selucid foundation of four major cities in that area helped a great deal in consolidating that holding, and constituted a tacit admission that the waves of Macedonian reinforcements that Alexander had been able to command had ceased and must be substituted by colonization, if power and influence over any area were to be maintained. Further west, in Asia Minor and Thrace, Antigonus assumed kingship, only to be supplanted after his death in the battle of Ipsus in 301, by Lysimachus who had been Alexander's former bodyguard and tutor. In Macedon itself, Cassander did his part to maintain the escalating level of atrocity and mayhem, managing to systematically destroy Alexander's wife Roxanne, their infant son, his mother Olympias and most of her relatives before his own death in 297 AD.

In the midst of all this violence and chaos, a remarkable civic phenomenon occurred on the Aegean coast of Asia Minor, where a man named Philetairos was granted guardianship over the considerable treasure of Lysimachus. Frantically trying to bide time until local alliances could be formed which would allow him to keep the bequest, Philetairos dissembled in ways that would easily rival Penelope's delay of her suitors. His delaying tactics having been successful, Philetairos began to expand his new city of Pergamon around the acropolis where the treasure had originally been stored, and in order to ensure the continued growth of the urban seeds he had planted with such great difficulty and skill, he named his nephew, Eumenes, as his successor. Eumenes continued to face threats, especially from the Seleucids, and during his twenty-two year reign continued the work his uncle had begun by expanding the scope and territory of the fledgling city. Upon the succession of Attalos I in 241 BC, the Attalid dynasty in Pergamon had finally become established as a strong independent principality in the midst of the constant fluctuations that then characterised the Hellenistic world.

During the brief period of its ascendency, Pergamon developed into what may be considered the prime example of a Hellenistic city, reflecting the highest aspirations of that highly underrated time. As such, the city offers a diametrically valid counterpoint to Classical Athens in both its design and mental self-images, providing a revealing contrast between two highly distinct periods in the process.

At the height of its power, Athens represented the concept of the polis as perhaps no other Classical Greek city had before; epitomising an independent city-state that could provide with its own resources everything its citizens could possibly want, and demanding total and absolute loyalty in return. Athena Polias, as the patron goddess of the city, was the supernatural personification of everything that this particular city-state had to offer, freeing its people from what Vincent Scully has called "their terror of the natural world with its dark powers and limited laws."[5]

In this way, civitas, as the basis of both civilisation and civic co-operation, represented the banding together of people in the most basic sense for their mutual self-interest, against uncertainties of the unknown, which were impossible to face alone. The actual physical, architectural form of Athens began, and continued to grow, in direct response to this view of the city as protector and provider. The "double nucleus" of agora and acropolis that also came to characterise many other Greek city states, here became a pragmatic division of both the sacred and profane division of civic life.[6] The Athenian agora, in its first century of existence, quickly evolved from a rather disorderly single file row of governmental buildings strung along the bottom of a low ridge to an encompassing parallelogram of both municipal and commercial structures deliberately placed to enclose a space intended for public gathering.[7] One of the most important determinants of the city's form, however, was the long established line of the Panathenaic procession. This was an annual pageant involving all the people of the city who joined together in an unspoken pledge to uphold the social contract into which each had willingly joined. The final destination of the procession, which was so integrally entwined into the social and architectural fabric of the city as to be immortalised in a frieze on the inner fascia of the Parthenon itself, was the acropolis, the home of Athena, the symbol of the city. The temple of the Parthenon and each of the other buildings around it thus had a profound meaning for all of the participants in the Panathenaia, as they approached the architectural ensemble through the frame of the Propalaia Gate. As Le Corbusier perceptively noted in remarking on the overwhelming force of the unified composition of all of the elements on the acropolis, "The whole thing ... provides vistas of a subtle kind; the different masses of the building being in an asymmetrical arrangement to create an intense rhythm. The whole composition is massive, elastic, living, terribly sharp and keen and dominating."[8] In addition, he quite rightly identifies the three-quarter perspective view of the Parthenon on the right and the Erectheum on the left, as leading the eyes of those approaching through the Propalaia directly toward the statue of Athena, which was placed between them on a projecting terrace to make it even more prominent. This theme of visual linkages has also been researched in depth by Constantine Doxiades, who has convincingly shown a direct mathematical relationship between the angle of vision of a viewer standing at the Propalaia and the location of the corners of the buildings flanking the statue of Athena. He has also gone on to apply this system to many other sites as well, with equally impressive results. The intricate relationship of the buildings on the Athenian acropolis then, as finally visualised by Pericles, Ictinus, Callicrates and Phidias in 432 BC, shows an intentional emphasis on the formation of external spaces. These were formed in a way that was directly related to group processions, and upon the specific impact of a prearranged point in those spaces upon the participants in that procession so that it might both achieve a religious experience and remind them of their common social bond.

Two centuries later however, in the incremental design of Attalid Pergamon, all of those factors had altered, and the perfect architectonic union between the people and their city had been critically changed. Because of the unique circumstances surrounding its founding and the need for the city to quickly become a viable political entity among the fragmented factions then vying for power, Pergamon did not have the luxury of a slow formal evolution that Athens enjoyed. Having experienced the greatest phase of its growth in the relatively brief thirty-eight year reign of Eumenes II, the instant city, which also had to deal with much more severe topographical demands, grew from the top down instead of in two directions at once.

From the initial nucleus of its acropolis, Pergamon expanded in widening terraces that cascaded down a steep mountainside toward the utilitarian marketplace of the lower city at its base. In telling contrast to Athens, pride of place in Pergamon is not given to a supernatural personification of the city but rather to the Attalid palaces which bring the concept of the city around in a full circle to its Mycenean beginnings. As at the start of the polis at that time, the fate of the people is put once again into the hands of men and not the gods.

The Trajan temple, or Trajaneum, which was placed nearby by the Romans, still forms a linear visual terminus to the spiralling arc of the city today, with the towering shell of its foundation wall standing as an architectural punctuation mark to the dramatic curve of the city. Built into a sheer cliff ledge, it is a symbolic finale to the fashionable trend toward royal deification begun soon after Alexander's death, when the boundary line between the attributes of gods and mortals in the Hellenic mind became hopelessly blurred by his larger than life exploits. The statue of Athena at Pergamon was not the climactic experience that rewarded a long expectant procession to her as in Athens, but is instead a secondary civic episode surrounded by a library, which is the real temple of the Hellenistic age. With its promise of fresh knowledge this library, like Pergamon itself, offered everyone the chance to look beyond the confines of the isolated citadel to the excitement of a rapidly changing and expanding world. Classical Athens, with all its promise, reach and dominion, had never been able to offer such a view.

Pergamene use of sculpture in the Athena sanctuary, as well as along the base of the great altar of Zeus, also tells this story very graphically, being used as it was for political purposes rather than to glorify the gods. As in the past, continual attacks by marauding bands of Gauls, who had traditionally exacted tribute from the territory to which Pergamon now laid claim, as well as continual threats from the Seleucids, Bithynians, Macedonians and others, meant that the Attalids were always forced to couple military might with public relations in order to survive. The pathos of the "Dying Gaul" sculptures that were strategically placed in the area around the Athena sanctuary and have survived in various Roman copies since, had therefore a purpose that went far beyond the use of sculpture to depict myth as it had done in the past. Here the groupings convey quite different levels of meaning by not only showing the supremacy of a beleaguered city over a ferocious and persistent enemy but also the honour due to a people who fought for what they felt to be their right. Both levels of meaning contributed to the strong political stance taken by Pergamon, in which the desire for peace with honour was backed with a willingness to fight, if necessary, to protect the city from all invaders. In this stance there was the important recognition that public opinion both inside and outside the city walls was important and could be positively affected by the use of symbols. The gigantomachy that forms the frieze around the base of the altar of Zeus intentionally conveys the idea of a struggle of epic, almost melodramatic proportions, reflecting a feeling of constant danger and possible extinction that all those in the city may have felt. As a sacrificial altar on a grand scale it was a place where animals would be routinely slaughtered at the base of its stairway and then be carried up onto the 12 metre long table within to be presented to Zeus. High political visibility and events that combined expanded opportunity with great risk, seemed to bring out grandiose statements such as this in Pergamon and led to the immortalisation of the altar as the "Throne of Satan" in the Biblical Book of Revelation.[9] The effectiveness of such statements was not lost upon the Romans who followed, as they also sought to develop an architecture that would impress and subjugate those whom they ruled. At Pergamon, as Vincent Scully has said, "self aggrandising human calculations seem perhaps all too obviously to make the city's deity a complex expression of human contrivance. Thus her physical reality was not so firmly embodied as it was at the classic site, where the Parthenon, though already explicitly involved with what men wanted to be, was still a demanding being, uniquely and wholly itself, which gave special meaning to all the other forms and relationships through the terror and wonder of its presence."[10] The Red Hall, or Kizel Avlu, which is such a presence in the midst of the old town of Bergama today, was the Temple of Serapis, a Graeco-Egyptian deity which blended eastern and western influence in typically Hellenistic fashion (plate 28). Standing at roughly the halfway point between the centre of ancient Pergamon and the idyllic pine grove that now surrounds the Aesclepion outside the city, the Red Hall effectively spans what had been called the Selinus River that runs below it, the symbol of death and the underworld for the Romans. In addition to these past architectural riches Bergama today is a carpet-making centre that generously supplies many shops throughout the town. This constant display of brightly coloured wool can be very distracting for those single-minded individuals who are only interested in the ruins on the hill, but for those in the market for a carpet, this is a paradise.

Foça, or Phocala as it was known in classical times, lies at the tip of a small peninsula around the bay of Çandarli from Bergama and is a picture-book fishing village wrapped around its protective harbour that has, along with its neighbours Datça and Çeşme, some of the most memorable vernacular architecture and beautiful beaches on the Aegean Coast (plate 29). From Foça it is possible to follow the Gediz river and the Kavaklidere Valley, which produces some of Turkey's finest wines, to Sardis and the heart of the ancient Kingdom of Lydia. Manisa, which is halfway between the colourful market town of Menemen and Sardis, was highly regarded by all of the diverse cultures of Anatolia, who have left their mark there (plate 30).

The Manisa Ulu Cami which was built under the auspices of the Sanuhanid principality in 1336, and the Muradiye Complex of Murad III, who chose the city as a retreat in 1444 because of its mystic leanings, make a study of each of these buildings worthwhile en route to Sardis. Archaeological investigation into "Golden Sardis" is relatively new, and has revealed that it was a large city, covering nearly 250 acres with a population of between 25,000 and 50,000 people. This was the ancestral home of the kings of Lydia beginning with Gyges in 680 BC, followed in turn by Andys, Sadyattes, Alyattes and finally Kroisos (or Croesus as he is known in the West), who ruled from 560 to 546 BC. The extensive mining of gold here from the Pactolus River between 600 and 550 BC gave Sardis the reputation of being the richest city in the ancient world and has also guaranteed Croesus immortality as history's richest king. As the first kingdom to perfect a system of state guaranteed coinage, Lydia's wealth soon began to attract outside attention, leading to the invasion and conquest of Sardis by Ionian Greeks in 499 BC.[11] The general outline of the city as it continues to emerge seems to follow the typical Hellenic format in Asia Minor, where as Professor George Hanfmann has said, the Greeks "pioneered the kind of city planning that was to be carried to Egypt and Africa and then through Asia to India by Alexander the Great and his successors".[12] The standard formula used in this planning typically included a civic agora in a lower zone, where commercial activity took place, that was separate from the agora on a promontory, acting as a citadel for both palace and temple. In Sardis, there were slight deviations from this model in that high walls seem to have divided the city into wards, and two royal palaces were split between the acropolis and the agora. King Croesus, who may or may not have played an active role in the design of Sardis, is known to have done so in both archaic Assos and Ephesus, where his interest in the work of the Greek geometer, Thales, is evident.[13] Extensive gymnastic and bathing complexes have been unearthed in Sardis, as has an enormous synagogue. A seating capacity of nearly 1000 in the latter has led to the conclusion that there was a large and wealthy Jewish community here during the time of the Roman empire (plate 31). The temple of Artemis, which is one of the best preserved of the classical buildings on the site, was originally dedicated to the Anatolian goddess Cybele, but was re-dedicated to her Hellenic counterpart, when Alexander came to the town on his way through Asia Minor. This temple, and the necropolis of the Lydian kings, called Bin Tepe by the Turks, are all that now remain to give substance to the legend of King Croesus.

Returning to the coast, the road to the port of Çeşme goes through Izmir, which is Turkey's third largest city. This large industrialised area gives little hint of its classical past as Smyrna, which was one of the most important cities in the Graeco-Roman world. The turbulence of the Aegean here prevented the port from silting up and so kept it in continuous use, ensuring both its progressive development and the total obliteration of most archaeological remains. As the scene of a Greek invasion in 1920, the memory of Izmir has had many painful associations for the Turks, who pushed the Greeks back into the sea here in 1922.

Çeşme, which means "fountain" in Turkish, is a convenient resort area for people living in Izmir, who come to enjoy the fine beaches, clear blue water and the thermal springs. The town itself, which lies in sight of the Greek island of Chios, centres around a 14th century Genoese fortress, and the newly restored Çeşme caravanserai next to it. Re-opened by the Altin Yünus or Golden Dolphin group, which also owns a fine contemporary hotel on a long stretch of beach on the way out of town, the caravanserai was originally built during the reign of Sultan Süleyman. Caravanserais, or inns for passing caravans, were intended as safe havens for the protection of trade goods, usually at forty kilometre (or nine hours by camels' pace) intervals, along the caravan route. Throughout the 13th century, Seljuk sultans built caravanserais along the two main commercial routes that bisected Anatolia from east to west and north to south, which were later carefully administered by the Ottomans, who passed legislation strictly controlling their use. The restoration of this caravanserai gives a good idea of the character of the interior space, even though the function has now entirely changed.

The village of Sigalik, which is close to Çeşme, is another long defunct village with a glorious classical past. Previously known as Teos, it was once large enough to have been considered the leader of all of the cities in the Ionian League, and Alexander the Great even proposed linking it to the Bay of Izmir with a canal across the peninsula which is here at its narrowest. One of the infinitely fascinating threads in the complex web of Turkish history is that a citizen of this city, named Apellikon, may have been single-handedly responsible for saving many of the original manuscripts of Aristotle. Having bought the entire library of the philosopher in 100 BC, he later saw that it was given intact to the Roman general, Sulla. Sulla in turn entrusted the publication of many of the manuscripts to a scholar named Tyrannian, and it was these copies that served as the basis of the study of Aristotle's work throughout the Middle Ages.[14]

Perhaps one of the hallmarks of a great city is that it can mean many different things to different people at several levels. Using that criteria Ephesus was, and still is, a great city, as it continues to engage almost everyone who visits it. From Çeşme it is only a short distance to what is called Efes today. Efes is an increasingly popular destination because of the great visual impact of the original monuments and the calibre of the restoration work now underway there. From fantastic foundation myths involving Amazons to life as a Hittite city named Apasas, invasion by Thracian Sea People, rule by the legendary King Croesus, Persian occupation, liberation by Alexander the Great, visits by Anthony and Cleopatra and finally Biblical associations with St Paul, St John and the Virgin Mary, few cities are able to claim such an illustrious history and famous company. As for the Amazons, the foundation myth involving them may not have been so fantastic considering that many corroborating stories about a tribe of fierce female warriors from the Black Sea coast still exist in Turkey. They remained an important part of the

Ephesian consciousness, just as the Gauls did in Pergamon, perhaps because of their strong principles, or because Ephesus, like Pergamon had the need for an honourable foe to give it greater legitimacy. Because local legends of the slaughter of Amazons in front of the Temple of Artemis by invading Greeks continued to survive, a famous competition was organised to immortalise their courage. According to the historian Pliny, famous Greek sculptors such as Phidias, Polykleitos and Kresilas were invited to Ephesus in 435 BC to compete in the creation of a grouping to be placed in front of the archaic temple there to commemorate the massacre, in a striking parallel to the kinds of sculptural groupings of Gauls used at Pergamon. It was the Pax Romana of Augustus that gave Ephesus both the time and the prosperity to develop fully, and much of what is visible there today is from this period. The temple of Hadrian, which is an unmistakable reminder of Roman influence, uses a delicate bust of Tyche as the keystone of its entry arch, and there is no doubt that Tyche, as the goddess of chance, had special significance for a city that looked back to a past filled with so many upheavals (plate 32).

A change of emphasis in city government under the Romans, from popular control to rule by the wealthy class only, led to a pattern of civic donations that eventually benefited almost every city in Asia Minor.[15] The Celsus Library and the Vedius Gymnasium in Ephesus are two such bequests that greatly enhanced the prestige of the city, and the library is especially well preserved today (plate 33). Located at a highly visible point at the crossing of two important streets, the Celsus Library was designed to cleverly use the "Scenea" architecture usually associated with Roman stage backdrops to both expand an elevation that had originally been restricted by neighbouring buildings and to use a metaphor which the public would automatically associate with the theatre. In doing so, the design seems to entice the public to come through the screen, to become participants in the wider drama waiting backstage. Statues placed in the projecting niches flanked by columns represent the virtues of Sophia, Episteme, Ennoaia and Arete, commemorating the wisdom, knowledge, destiny and intellect of Celsus, whose mausoleum was also located here.

Ephesus, which diagonally inserts itself between the Bulbul Daği (Mt Coressos) and Panayir Daği (Mt Pion) relates to both the agora and the theatre in its centre, which were the spaces closest to the daily activities of the people. The theatre itself is most famous as the scene of the riot that followed St Paul's speech there in 53 AD, when he was in Ephesus to organise its first Christian church (plate 34). Economics then, as now, were integral to religion, and were the real issue behind the riot which was begun by artisans who felt their trade in statues of Artemis was threatened. When they shouted "Great is Artemis Ephesia" they really meant to say that "great are the profits that we get from making souvenirs for visitors to her temple." Ironically, it was also the ancient belief in Artemis in this part of Anatolia that eased the progress of Christianity, since people could easily make a mental transition from Artemis to the Virgin Mary, who accompanied St John here from Patmos. The first church dedicated to her stills stands, having been built over the ruins of an elongated, secular building called the Hall of Muses. The Third Ecumenical Council was also held here in 431 AD, ironically debating whether Mary, who according to tradition lived at the top of Mt Coressos, some 6 kilometres away, was mortal, immortal, or both. A visit to this house, which has now been sanctioned by the Catholic Church as having been hers, convinces even the most hardened sceptic, not necessarily through the written evidence offered, or the visions quoted, or the historical accuracy or inaccuracy of its architectural style, but simply through the pervasive peace of the place itself. The resort of Kuşadasi, or Bird Island nearby, offers a striking contemporary contrast to the ancient grandeur of Efes, and is now beginning to become the Aegean equivalent to cosmopolitan centres such as Bodrum, Marmaris and Antalya on the Mediterranean Coast. Somehow the hectic pace of the nightlife here makes the conversion into a discotheque of the fortress on the island which gives the city its name seem quite logical. The Hotel Kismet, or the Mehmet Paşa Caravanserai, which is similar to the one in Çeşme, make comfortable stopping points from which to organise another inland foray eastward through Aydin to Aphrodisias and Pammukale, as well as south to Priene, Miletus, Didyma, Lake Bafa and Milas.

Aphrodisias, which is about a two hour drive from Kuşadasi, is near Geyre in the heart of what was ancient Caria, at the base of the Baba Dağ mountains. Little historical information exists about it other than numismatic evidence and mention of the city in several decrees issued by Julius Caesar (plate 35). Architectural evidence indicates that after the death of Christ this was a stubborn pocket of paganism due to close association with the goddess who was its namesake. Arab and Seljuk raids later forced the total evacuation of the city, which greatly helped to preserve it. Known to be the centre of the arts, with its School of Aphrodisias, it attracted visits by such luminaries as the sculptor Praxiteles, and re-interpretations of classical Greek statues done here were sent all over the world. The site itself is enormous, covering nearly 520 hectares of mostly flat ground. The temple of Aphrodite, which was one of her most enduring sanctuaries, was later converted into a basilica by a persistent Christian church. The Cotton Fortress of Pamukkale, which is one hour further on, had been known as Hieropolis in antiquity and is in reality a series of petrified cascades of calcium oxide, holding pools of bubbling, thermal water (plate 36). Hieropolis was named after Hiera, who was also involved in the foundation legend of Pergamon, thus establishing a link between this city and the Attalid Kingdom. Like so many recently uncovered sites in Turkey, the city was virtually unknown until German excavations revealed it in 1898.

The southern route from Kuşadasi, through Söke, leads first to the Hellenistic city of Priene, which is carved in a steep precipice called Samsun Dağ, near the village of Gullubache (plate 37). Priene has no equal as an example of the blind application of the Hippodamian gridplan, which was used here regardless of the condition of the terrain. A network of streets set at right angles was set up, using an agora, theatre and temple as a centre, and a circling wall was thrown around it, climbing dizzily up the mountainside. In spite of the severe rigidity of the planning principle used, a southern orientation was chosen, to allow maximum sunlight, and the grid system is not as intrusive as it might seem, when walking through the town, since breathtaking views divert attention from it.

A similar plan was used in the layout of Miletus nearby to much greater effect since the land there is totally flat. The only irregularity to be dealt with was the jagged outline of what has been a large peninsula projecting into the gulf of Lade, which had since silted up. Edmund Bacon has done an excellent analysis of the ingenious variety achieved within this grid in Miletus, showing that in spite of the inherent sterility of the system, creative breakthroughs are possible.[16] The Ilyas Bey Mosque near Miletus is an architectural gem that should not be missed. Built in 1404, by a ruler of the same name belonging to the Menteşoğüllari principality, the mosque is located in the village of Balat, close to the border with Aydin. The single domed, square plan building stands out as one of the most attractive mosques of this type built before the Ottoman ascendency (plate 38).

Lake Bafa, which is east of Miletus, was originally a deep inlet of the Aegean which was eventually closed off by the same unpredictable changes of the Maeander River that sealed the fate of Priene and Miletus as well. The fortress of Heracleia, which was built by Lycemachos at the base of Mt Latmos, stretches out along the shore of the lake (plate 39). Christian priests coming from the Sinai Peninsula and Yemen established monasteries here in the 7th century, and many of these can still be seen scattered over many of the islands in the lake. West of Bafa, the Temple of Didyma, which was under the control of the city of Miletus, offers a rare and remarkably accurate construct of the Hellenistic mind in microcosm (plate 40). The building is treated as a plastic object in the landscape, as in the past, but is a temple within a temple, in which an ideal inner landscape is created as an idyllic alternative to the politically and physically harsh world outside the walls of the sanctuary (plate 41). To achieve this deception, the scale of the outer shell of the temple is first made enormous, and at 167ft x 358ft (50.9m x 109.1m) is the third largest structure in Hellenistic times after the Artemesion at Ephesus and the Hera temple on Samos.[17] Within this perimeter a man-made forest of breathtakingly slender Doric columns is used to surround a massive cella that, in dramatic variance to tradition, is open to the sky and oriented on an east-west axis to receive light all day long. The naiskos, or home of Apollo, was placed within this cliff-like enclosure, the head of this sacred spring and one of the most revered of his oracles after those at Delos and Delphi. Just as the Athenian Parthenon was the final goal of an annual pilgrimage of a city in celebration of itself, the Didymaon of Apollo is all about the journey of a single soul and the successive frustrations and discoveries made in the course of that journey. Didyma is a petrified intellectual world that represents the architectural equivalent of a play within a play, where symbols, scale and sequence are cleverly used to tell a story. In a way that is reminiscent of the Egyptian temple form which may have partially influenced it, and which became well known at that time due to Ptolemy's influence there; the worshipper, after ascending seven steps, first penetrates a porch of very high columns set deep; only to be confronted with a doorway fronting a stage set five feet above the level of the porch that effectively blocks further direct progress. This was the chresmographion, where the oracles of Apollo were announced by the priest of the temple. Because of the widespread renown of this oracle throughout the Hellenistic world this priest was also an important official in the nearby city of Miletus which had titular control over the temple. From this point, the worshipper could not see further into the temple itself, but only upward to the sky beyond, barely visible through the open cella. This contrast of dark and light not only had a highly symbolic significance, but also encouraged further exploration and movement inward, through channels called labyrinths, flanking the raised chresmographion, that led down into the sacred court, or adyton. At the extreme end of this adyton, which was planted with symmetrical rows of fragrant bay trees, stood the Temple of Apollo, seen primarily in elevation from whichever of the temple tunnels were chosen as an entrance. The temple was a relatively small architectural gem in the Ionic order set against the towering Corinthian pilasters supporting the sheer walls of the surrounding cella. The vegetal Corinthian capitals that crowned the top of these pilasters blended with those on a cornice running continuously around the rim of this man-made canyon. They served to soften both its hard edge and reinforce the imagery of natural power tempered with lushness begun by the masonry dado and grove of bay trees below.

The temple, as Vincent Scully has said, "is calculated to set up a baroque drama of basic sensations in the mind of the observer. The emotions so aroused must have made the complex nature of Apollo almost fully comprehensible; shelter and coolness in this grove, the taste of death in the dark restriction of his caves, release from the darkness once again into the trapped sunlight of the court with its whispering leaves."[18]

In this way, the labyrinthine tunnel is a parallel for the rite of passage of life itself, leading from the frustrating and confusing choices of this life into the crystalline clarity and perfect, symmetrical order of the next, where lush green forests, bubbling springs, ever present heaven and the eternal companionship of the gods are all that exist.

The city of Milas is located just before Bodrum, which is acknowledged to be the turning point from the Aegean to the Mediterranean region. The most memorable thing about the city is the Firuz-Bey Mosque, which is widely acknowledged for its fine workmanship and richness of materials (plate 42). Built in 1394 by Hoca Firuz-Bey, who was a governor of this region under Sultan Bayezit, it is called the Blue Mosque locally because of the overall impression given by the tiles there. Milas, once named Mylasa after a descendant of the sea god Poseidon, serves as a fitting conclusion to a region so closely connected to both the treasure and the terrors that the Aegean has brought to it.

Notes

1 For an extensive description of each of the levels, see: Akurgal, Ekrem, *Ancient Civilizations and Ruins of Turkey*, Istanbul, 1985, p. 48.

2 Betancourt, P. P., *The Aeolic Style in Architecture*, Princeton, 1977, is an important contribution to a thorough understanding of the beginnings of the Ionian style. For Neandria also see: Akurgal, E., op. cit., pp. 62–64.

3 Scully, Vincent, *The Earth, the Temple and the Gods*, New Haven, 1969, p. 170.

4 See: Jones, A. H. M., *The Greek City from Alexander to Justinian*, Oxford, 1984, for the effects of this population shift.

5 Scully, Vincent, op. cit., p. 171.

6 See Wycherley, R. E., *How the Greeks Built Cities*, New York, 1969.

7 For the best visual description of this remarkable transition, see: Bacon, Edmund, *Design of Cities*, New York, 1967.

8 Le Corbusier, *Toward a New Architecture*, Paris, 1922, p. 26.

9 Holy Bible, New International version, New Brunswick, N. J., 1978, Revelation 2:12, p. 742.

10 Scully, Vincent, op. cit., p. 197.

11 Hanfmann, George, *From Croesus to Constantine*, Ann Arbor, 1975, p. 6.

12 Ibid., p. 24.

13 Ibid., p. 10.

14 Akurgal, Ekrem, op. cit., p. 139.

15 Jones, A. H. M., op. cit.; gives a thorough analysis of the growing civic reliance upon personal donations.

16 Bacon, Edmund, op. cit.

17 Akurgal Ekrem, op. cit., p. 226.

18 Scully, Vincent, op. cit., p. 130.

CHAPTER III
THE MEDITERRANEAN COAST

The Mediterranean, which is called the "Ak Deniz" or "White Sea" by the Turks, serves as both a psychological and geographic mirror image of the "Kara Deniz" or Black Sea that makes up the country's northern border. The Aegean, the wine dark sea of Homer, seems opaque in comparison to the brilliance of this water, which is infinitely varied in its range from morning until evening. The colour of the water is not the only contrast between the Aegean and Mediterranean regions, as the latter has the hot summers and mild winters that other countries around this sea share. The effect of this warmer climate on the vegetation of the region is also dramatic, supporting pine forests, citrus groves, banana plantations, vivid pink wild oleanders, myrtle, rosemary and bay. The third important contrast with its Aegean neighbour is a direct result of the fact that this region was relatively isolated from the Hellenic migration that had such a telling effect in the west, meaning that indigenous Anatolian cultures here had a longer time to develop before Alexander's sweep east in 334 BC. A feeling of fierce independence pervades many of the ruins of the cities, which were occupied in the past by peoples of highly individualized traditions and languages. As proselytes of Hellenism after Alexander almost singlehandedly introduced it into Asia Minor, they redirected this zeal for independence into becoming more Greek than the Greeks.

Moving from west to east, the Mediterranean coast has historically been divided into five natural districts due to the undulations of the Tarsus mountains at its flank. Caria, as the first of these, centred primarily around the Bodrum peninsula, which thrusts itself westward like a horse's head and acts as a geographical demarcation between the two seas. Lycia, to the east of Caria, takes its name from Lykos, which is the Greek word for wolf, which seems to have some connection with the rugged wilderness here caused by the Tarsus mountains coming close to the sea. Confined more or less to a semi-circular section of coastline, Lycia extends from Fethiye on the west to Antalya on the east. Pamphylia, or "the land of tribes", is the third section of coastline falling roughly in the middle of the shore, consisting of a broad, flat, arable plain created by the recession of the Tarsus mountains inland.[1] Running from Antalya to Anamur, this arc-shaped coast creates a natural harbour, with Antalya as its main port. At Anamur, the Tarsus chain snakes toward the coast once again forming what the Romans had called 'Rough Cilicia', which is similar to Lycia in character, but even more spectacularly mountainous. Finally, at the eastern extreme of the coastline the mountains swing inland once again creating another fertile stretch of land that had been known as Cilicia, with Adana now in its centre.

A fourth difference between the Aegean and the Mediterranean coasts is the larger number of cosmopolitan cities in the south, due perhaps to its early accessibility to the rest of the ancient world as part of the Roman province of Asia. Bodrum, which was known as Halikarnassos, is an anomaly in this conservative country, having taken on a jet-set reputation as the hot-spot of the Turkish Riviera (plate 43). The naturally protected port here, which has always been one of the major attractions of the city, has now made Bodrum a large yachting centre, and the perfect starting point for a "blue-tour" on a Turkish *gület*, or wooden boat, along the coast. Chartering a Bodrum boat for a tour can involve anything from a day trip to one lasting several weeks, depending on finances, whim, and time available. Seeing the coast from the water, punctuated by brief anchorages to explore the shore, offers an entirely new perspective on this region of the country where the coastline has only now begun to be altered by the hand of man.

The Turkish *gület* is wider than a normal yacht and therefore has a flatter deckspace, allowing it to comfortably handle up to twelve people on a group charter, with meals prepared on board by the crew. One of the typical trips from Bodrum is the sail to Kara Ada, or the Black Island, which has many hidden beaches and grottos all along its coast. On land, a network of roads that invite exploration branch out from Bodrum, such as the 30 kilometre stretch to the west that leads to the village of Gümüslük, at the tip of the peninsula. Myndos, which has long since been submerged, is clearly visible beneath the crystal clear water here, completely preserved in its liquid grave.[2]

Bodrum itself is perhaps best known for a monument that has not been so fortunate since it has now totally vanished. The Mausoleum of Halikarnassos, which has since given its name to any burial structure with pretensions of grandeur, was a marble mountain erected in memory of King Mausolus of Caria, by his wife Artemisia in 350 BC. Although speculation about its appearance continues because nothing but fragments of a frieze from the original structure remain, its general form has been agreed upon.

The Mausoleum was a huge, tripartite wedding cake of a building, with a relatively thin base, a high, shaft-like middle section, and a colonnaded, pyramidically roofed top, capped with a statue of Mausolus in a chariot that could be seen for miles around. Nearly 140 feet in height, the tomb was further decorated by friezes depicting events from the king's life, done by many of the best sculptors of the time.

The focal point of Bodrum today has shifted to the Castle of St Peter on an island in the middle of its harbour. The castle, which dates from 1402, was built by the Knights of St John, who used much of the material from the Mausoleum in its construction. The castle, which was later taken over by the Ottomans, today houses the Bodrum Archaeological Museum, which is divided into three sections. The Mycenae Hall, which is the first of these, houses recent finds from Musgehi and Dirmil, mostly from the prehistoric period. The second section, called the underwater exhibit, is a unique display of finds taken from the ocean floor nearby, such as amphorae, glass and sponges, which give a vivid idea of maritime activity here in the past. The third section, called the Caria Hall is also important because it displays pieces of the eastern frieze of the Mausoleum, which is the only other sample that still exists besides that now in the British Museum.

The influence of Rhodes is very strong in this area, and the Marmaris peninsula, which is separated from Bodrum by the rare liquid amber forests of the Gokova Bay, is even closer to the island, to which it is connected by a regular ferry service. As the most protected harbour on the Mediterranean coast, Marmaris has recently experienced a level of popular activity similar to that of Bodrum, with a forest of yacht masts flying flags from all over the world, now lining its corniche. Like Bodrum, Marmaris makes a wonderful starting point for boating day-trips, and one of the best of these is to go on a trip through the flat reed beds of the Dalyan river delta and past the carved rock tombs that line the cliffs around the river, to the ruins of the city of Kaunos. Several other, longer excursions from Marmaris could involve trips to Datça and Knidos at the tip of the Marmaris peninsula to the west, or toward Fethiye to the east, which in either case will require more than a day.

Datça, like Assos, Çeşme and Foça on the Aegean coast, was a charming fishing village which has recently begun to gain popularity among tourists and locals alike, and whose uniqueness now threatens to change it. The ancient city of Knidos, which is further on down the peninsula at its tip, was once an important commercial centre best known for both its wine and a famous statue of Aphrodite by Praxiteles. While the remains of this city are not as impressive as some others, due to extensive removals, the synthesis of what still exists and the site itself, apparently isolated in the middle of the sea, most certainly is (plate 44). Fethiye, on the other hand, lies tucked inside a bay of the same name and was virtually inaccessible until a new road was built to it recently. As the westernmost bracket of the wilderness of Lycia which curves out from it, Fethiye has increasingly become the first stop on the way to the magnificent beaches of Ölü Deniz, fifteen kilometres away (plate 45). After first heading directly east to Kemer, this road then heads south toward the coast and the heartland of ancient Lycia. Moving past the spectacular rock tombs cut into the cliffs around Pinara (now called Minare Köyü) and the high acropolis of Tlos, which was used as a pirate stronghold until late in the 19th century, the road eventually comes to Xanthus, which was the capital of this region in the past. Having only come into public view in 1838, after the publication of the findings of Sir Charles Fellows following his excavations there, Xanthus epitomizes both the essential complexity and fierce independence of the Lycian name, and the remains seen today seem to fan out from a central stronghold that has repeatedly been the scene of tragic mass suicides in the past. The first of these occurred in 545 BC when Xanthus was invaded by the Persians who were led by general Harpagos during their conquest of Asia Minor. Rather than surrender to superior numbers, the Xanthian men immolated their families within the acropolis walls, and then burst out to die fighting. This scene was repeated in 42 BC when Brutus, who led the Roman expedition to Xanthus, is said to have wept at the bravery of his foe. The pillar tombs which anchor one end of the theatre standing near the acropolis today are of a type that is unique to Lycia, designed to be miniature versions of the village houses as a perpetual home for the dead (plate 46).

Xanthus is best remembered today as the original home of the Nereid Monument which is now one of the most popular exhibits in the British Museum. Designed in the form of an Ionic temple placed on a high podium, the monument bears two sets of reliefs showing battle scenes, and has four main columns supporting an architrave and pediment. Each of the three column bays frame a statue of the Nereids from whom the monument is named, and each of these statues is uncharacteristically fluid in style, seeming to be constantly commanding an invisible gale.

Further on from Xanthus, past the sanctuary of Leto and the important Roman port of Patara, the main road from Fethiye curves eastward along the coastline through Kas and Kalkan to Aperlae, on Kekova Island (plate 47). Marking the mid-way point around the Lycian curve into the Mediterranean, this island is a long, thin spit of land separated from the mainland by a narrow channel of shallow crystal blue water that barely covers the ruins of the city of Aperlae, since claimed by the sea. Partially or totally submerged sarcophagi, as well as fragments of Byzantine churches, litter the shores here, showing to what extent its position has changed over the centuries, and bringing the temporality of human efforts graphically home once again. This same sense of temporality is also conveyed by the shell of a small Byzantine church on the banks of the Kokarkay river at Demre, now Deragzi, nearby (plate 48).

Having been recently discovered, it is now the focus of scholarly attention due to its unusual form.[3] Myra and Demre are more famous as the home of St Nicholas, and the origin of the legend of Santa Claus, or Noel Baba as the Turks call him. As the Bishop of Myra in the 4th century, Nicholas began providing dowries for girls from poor families in the village, who could not have married otherwise.

Because his prayers were also felt to have saved the lives of the seamen who were caught in a storm while taking Nicholas across the Mediterranean to Palestine, he is now the patron saint of sailors as well. The bishop's tomb is inside a church in Myra that bears his name, even though his remains have long since been removed by a raiding party from Bari, who took them to Italy in 1087 (figures 17, plan, and 18, perspective).

Antalya, which is the easternmost bracket of Lycia, and has about ten times the population of its western counterpart Fethiye, is undeniably one of the most important port cities in this region. When Pergamon took over the neighbouring district of Pamphylia, the city was ceded to Rome after the death of the last of the Attalid kings. Many of the ruins seen there today, such as the magnificently well preserved Hadrian's Gate, are a reminder of the long and prosperous period of Roman rule here. This particular gate has been especially successful in making a transition in the 20th century, as it now seems to be the focus of the social life of many of the young people in the area, when they come to the centre of the city. The profusion of Byzantine ruins here, like those of the Panagic church, (later converted into the Korkud mosque by a son of Bayezit II), also testifies to the continuing importance of the city during that time (plate 49).

The "Antalya Citadel and Marina Leisure Centre" project, just recently completed, has particularly benefited the oldest section of the city, where narrow winding alleyways sloping down toward the crowded marina at the bottom of the hill are lined with countless colourful shops. The Hotel Turban Adalya here, which was first built as the branch office of an Istanbul bank in 1869, later fell on hard times as a warehouse. A good example of the success of the citadel project, the building has today been restored as a stylish hotel in the midst of the frenetically active old city, and is a comfortable place from which to explore it, as well as sites on this side of Lycia and in Pamphylia to the east.

Just as in Fethiye, it is possible to walk along the quay of the old port of Antalya and negotiate a day trip boat charter with several owners, prior to the day of departure. From Antalya, an especially rewarding trip is to go from the old port

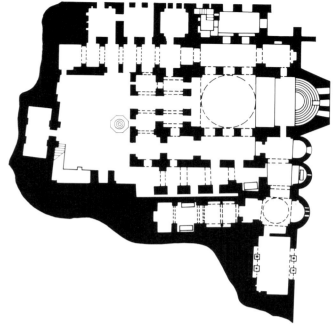

Figure 17 Church, Demre.

Figure 18 St. Nicholas Church, axonometric.

down along the eastern shore of Lycia toward the ruins of Phaesilis nearly three hours away. Due to the unusual siting of the city on a small boot-shaped peninsula projecting into the sea, its main street, which is still virtually intact, spans two separate harbours and slightly changes direction at its agora to accomplish the link. Seen from its main entrance from the south harbour, which is where most yachts anchor because of its depth, Phaesilis is almost completely invisible behind a uniformly high and dense cover of pine trees that obscure it. Once up on the beach, and then to the steps that lock onto the wide marble paved cardo maximus however, the city structure starts to become legible, and the desire to discover where the main street leads become overwhelming.The northern harbour is smaller and far more enclosed than its opposite number, framing and turning the distant view from the cardo and rewarding the walk along it with a final liquid gift. Alexander the Great, who passed by here on his way east, was said to have been enchanted with Phaesilis, and walking along its pine scented cardo in high summer, with the sound of the cicadas grinding in the background and the green rimmed bay in the distance, it is neither difficult to place him here nor to understand why (plate 50).

A massive construction programme has been underway for some time in Turkey, in order to accommodate the steadily rising number of visitors who seem especially drawn to the Mediterranean coast. Because financial incentives are also being offered to development companies who are interested in building new hotels, there have been many extraordinary buildings produced, such as the Side Palace Hotel which has just opened. Thoroughly post-modern in style, this phantasmagoria is more than simply a place to stay, but is a lesson in Turkish architectural history all on its own. The designers have taken it upon themselves to make the complex a catalogue of every possible historical reference they can manage to fit in and somehow the entire composition not only works extremely well, but also offers stimulating challenges to the memory around every corner. In one direction are tall roof chimneys that recall those over the Topkapı Palace kitchens, here used to both cover and light the hotel dining room in a newly aesthetic and less utilitarian role. Various versions of the traditionally broad-eaved and wooden bracketed Turkish house here become sitting rooms projecting from the corners of the building, while smaller scale versions of several of Sinan's bridges span the main entrance driveway and act as open outside corridors to the rooms. Even long lost cousins are included in a reference to the Mamluks of Egypt, with pyramids covering both the bar and the discotheque. Far from being merely stage-set architecture, the hotel also functions very well, and is a welcome haven to return to after a day of exploring the surrounding countryside. The Pamphylian cities of Side, Perge and Aspendos nearby are each important and highly individual in their own right and all in a remarkably good state of preservation. The theatres in each of these three cities are especially interesting, with that of Aspendos being one of the best preserved classical theatres now in existence.

Specifically Roman in style, the completeness of the theatre at Aspendos provides a valuable image to remember when seeing the numerous other less well preserved examples in the area. The Roman habit of using an elaborate scenea and proscenium stage to focus attention on the drama and away from the surrounding landscape, has here left behind a virtually intact structure all its own, which is so grand that the Seljuks used it as a palace. It is easy to forget that all of the classical

Plate 1 Istanbul from the roof of the Hagia Sophia

Plate 2 Hagia Sophia

Plate 3 Hagia Eirene

Plate 4 Topkapı

Plate 5 Topkapı, Sultan's Reception Room

Plate 6 Topkapı tiles, Sunnet Odasi.

Plate 7 Sokullu Mehmet Pasha

Plate 8 Bayezit Mosque

Plate 9 Bayezit Square

Plate 10 Nurosmaniye Mosque

Plate 11 Süleymaniye Mosque

Plate 12 Fatih Cami

Plate 13 Zal Mahmut Paşa Mosque

Plate 14 Fatih Cami

Plate 15 Yeni Mosque

Plate 16 Houses, Arnavutköy

Plate 17 Rumeli Hisari

Plate 18 Wooden house, Anadolu Hisari, detail.

Plate 19 Bosphorus Bridge

Plate 20 Dolmabahçe Palace interior

Plate 21 Yildiz Palace

Plate 22 Nusretiye Mosque

Plate 23 Piyale Paşa Mosque

Plate 24 Yildirim Mosque, Bursa.

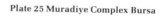

Plate 25 Muradiye Complex Bursa

Plate 26 Dome, Muradiye

Plate 27 Üç Şerefli Cami, Edirne.

Plate 28 The Kizel Avlu, Bergama, formerly a temple of Serapis.

Plate 29 The bay at Phocala

Plate 30 Manisa

Plate 31 Sardis

Plate 32 The temple of Hadrian at Ephesus

Plate 33 The library at Ephesus

Plate 34 The theatre at Ephesus

Plate 35 Aphrodisias

Plate 36 Pamukkale

Plate 37 Priene

Plate 38 Ilyas Bey Mosque, Miletus.

Plate 39 The fortress of Heracleia, Lake Bafa.

Plate 40 Medusa head near Didyma

Plate 41 Temple at Didyma

Plate 42 Firuz-Bey Mosque, Milas.

Plate 43 Bodrum

Plate 44 Knidos

Plate 45 Fethiye

Plate 46 Xanthus

Plate 47 Kekova

Plate 48 Deragzi

Plate 49 Korkud Cami

Plate 50 Phaesilis

Plate 51 Termessos

Plate 52 Manavgat

Plate 53 Alanya

Plate 54 Anamur

Plate 55 Tarsus Mountains

Plate 56 Yilani Kale

Plate 57 Anavarza Church

Plate 58 Munzur mountains and Tigris River

Plate 59 Harran, houses.

Plate 60 Harran, minaret of mosque.

Plate 61 Urfa, Abdurrahman mosque.

Plate 62 Urfa, Abdurrahman mosque.

Plate 63 Sultan Isa Medrese, Mardin.

Plate 64 Great Mosque, Diyarbakir.

Plate 65 Nemrut Dağ

Plate 66 Nemrut Dağ

Plate 67 Hasen Keyf Gate

Plate 68 Hasen Keyf, Zeynel-Bey Tomb.

Plate 69 Uzbek Turk

Plate 70 Local children at a festival

Plate 71 Hoşap Castle

Plate 72 Akhtamar Church

Plate 73 Halime Khatun Kumbet

Plate 74 Halime Khatun door plate

Plate 75 Bayindir Kumbet, Ahlat.

Plate 76 Erzurum Çifte Minare

Plate 77 Mama Khatun, Tercan

Plate 78 Mama Khatun, Tercan

Plate 79 Lion, Hattusas

Plate 80 Tomb, Eskişehir.

Plate 81 Arslankaya

Plate 82 Cappadocia

Plate 83 Cappadocia

Plate 84 Fresco, Karanlik.

Plate 85 Kaymakli

Plate 86 Elaziğ, Izzet Paşa Mosque.

Plate 87 Elaziğ, Izzet Paşa Mosque.

Plate 88 Malatya, Ulu Cami.

Plate 89 Gök Medrese, Siva

Plate 90 Divriği, portal.

Plate 91 Eşrefoğlu, Beyşehir.

Plate 92 Hagia Sophia, Trebizond.

Plate 93 Hagia Sophia, Trebizond.

Plate 94 Sumela Monastery

Plate 95 A colourful group of villagers

Plate 96 Saframbolu

Plate 97 Traditional house, Saframbolu

cities whose ruins cover Anatolia needed water to survive, and often invented ingenious ways of getting it. At Aspendos, the remains of an enormous aqueduct marching across the flat countryside toward the city on a high, table-top mesa above serves as a reminder of the extreme and difficult steps taken to provide this precious resource to the people. Termessos, which is 35 kilometres northwest of Antalya, and far less accessible than Perge, Side and Aspendos, is perched 1000 metres above sea level near the crest of Mt Gülluk on a series of terraces chosen for their great defensibility and view of the Yenice Pass below, which the city controlled. Originally founded by an indigenous people called the Solyms, the city is famous for its fierce independence in the past, as it is one of the few to have avoided occupation by Alexander the Great. After several unsuccessful sorties, the wise general determined that its capture would serve little purpose and would not be worth the high price in human life required to take it. Unlike Aspendos, the theatre at Termessos has a clear view of its surroundings which in this case includes the spectacular rock face of Mt Solym directly across from it, which is so high that it is often above the clouds (plate 51). One of the last of the classical cities of Anatolia to have been recently brought to light, Termessos, today remains relatively unknown, even though it is accessible by car and a part of the newly established Termessos National Park lies at its base. As such, it joins a select group of other cities in this region, such as Xanthus, Labranda and Arycanda, whose mysterious past, isolation, and adaptation to a different site make them an unforgettable experience.

The road along the coast from Antalya goes close to the Koprülü Canyon National Park, and Manavgat, which is a beneficiary of the waterfalls caused by the river coming from the canyon (plate 52). Alanya, to the west, near the far extreme of the Pamphylian plain where the Tarsus mountains swing back toward the sea is an appropriately fortified gateway to Rough Cilicia. Known to the Romans as Coracesium, it became a stronghold of sea-raiders who terrorized the Mediterranean due to its well defended harbours, the same Cilician pirates who captured Julius Caesar and St Paul. Many cities in this area signed treaties with these pirates in order to co-exist with them and Side was even known to have surrendered its port to them, as well as its market place, which was used for the sale of their slaves. The Roman Senate finally decided to take steps against them in 103 BC, and put Mark Antony in charge of the clean-up operation. Although he was able to achieve sizable victories on land, eventually leading to the establishment of the province of Cilicia, he was unable to totally eradicate the pirates who re-appeared several years later while the Romans were preoccupied with the war against the rebel Mithradates. The pirate fleet reached nearly one thousand ships at this time, and rampaged unchecked along the entire Mediterranean coast (plate 53).

Even Publius Serviluis Vatia, who managed to capture the fortress of the pirate leader Zeniketes in 78 BC and burn it down with him inside it, could not end the raids. While the fortifications of Alanya, which are now mixed with those of the Ottomans, are a testament to Roman persistence, the city of Anamur, once called Anemurium, is a monument to their obsession with death. Located on a desolate stretch of coastline directly across from Cyprus, the Roman city of the dead at Anemurium has survived largely because of its isolation (plate 54).

Detailed research into the peculiarities of this necropolis has shown that it differs widely from other Roman cemeteries in Italy and elsewhere in several important ways. First of all, the tombs are built of local, undressed limestone, rather than of the more ubiquitous marble seen elsewhere. The use of a local building material has led to the creation of new architectural forms on the mausolea, such as barrel vaulted chambers with benches, or arco solia on which to lay the dead, lining the inside, and more elaborate kinds of tombs. These involved the attachment of an ante-room, or walled court onto the front of the simple chamber, or even used a grouping of several chambers together into complexes that combined burial chambers with dining halls, apartments on upper stories, theatres, and pergolas from which to view the sea.[4] This gradual evolution from a city of the dead to one for both the living and the dead, along with the sheer scale at which this co-existence was achieved, make Anemurium a unique example of its type.

The stamp of the Crusades is indelibly marked out by the fortresses they left behind starting from Mut and Silifke, near Anamur. A gap in the Tarsus mountains called the Cilician Gates, near Kozan, and another through the Belen Pass to Antioch, made this a favoured route for armies moving eastward across central Anatolia toward Palestine, and also made the control of these passes strategically important (plate 55). Following the capture of Jerusalem by the various factions that combined to make up the First Crusade in 1099, and its recapture by Salah al-Din Ayub (or Saladin as he was known in the West) in 1187, another joint effort combining Frankish, English and French knights was launched. En route to Palestine, Frederick Barbarossa, the leader of the Franks drowned in the raging currents of the Göksu river near Silifke, throwing the other factions into confusion, and bringing this Crusade to an end.

The Yilani Kale, or Snake Fortress, which is in a mountain pass about eight kilometres north of the village of Ceyhan near Kozan, is a formidable legacy of this contentious time, standing guard over the broad grassy plain below (plate 56). While the Kiz Kalezi, near Silifke shares similar features with the Yilani Kale, and was said to have been built for the same purpose, local legend indicates otherwise. The castle, which also has a landward component, was supposedly built by a local Armenian ruler to protect his daughter from a fortune teller's prediction that she would die from a snakebite. The precaution was in vain, however, as a snake that had hidden itself in a basket of fruit sent to the castle by a suitor finally made the prediction come true.

The chaos of the Crusades, especially the capture of Constantinople by the Fourth Crusade in 1204, also ironically spawned many Byzantine monastic communities seeking to escape the conflagration. Coenobitical religious societies were set up in many inaccessible places throughout Anatolia, and the self-contained monastic villages around Kozan were a part of this movement. Alahan monastery, which is located about twenty kilometres north of Mut, is one of the most pre-eminent groupings of this kind, precariously carved into a terrace high above the Göksu river gorge.

Combining a large basilica, smaller church, refectory, kitchen and monks' cells into a single structure, this monastery, which is strung out in a long line against its high cliff, clearly conveys the precariousness of everyday existence at this time. Anavarza church, or Anazarbus, which is thirty kilometres north of Ceyhan, is a name said to derive from an Arabic phrase meaning "the source of the eye". The original name may have come from the destruction of this church by an earthquake in 526 BC, and its subsequently haunted appearance may have given the Arabs the impression that it was evil or the source of the evil eye.

The church was fortified by twenty towers, placed every seventy metres around its perimeter wall. This wall which varies in height from eight to ten metres, closely follows the configuration of the cliff on which it is built, making it and the rock beneath one (plate 57). At Kadirli, close to Kozan, the Sion Monastery, whose walls are now nearly all destroyed, follows the contours of its rocky perch, just as closely, seeming to fuse into the cliff that once protected it (figure 17).

These three monasteries, while only forming a small part of the entire movement throughout Anatolia, each show the general principles of self-sufficiency that were common to them all, and the use of adverse conditions to best advantage, in order to ensure survival.

In a country of unparalleled diversity and historical richness, the Mediterranean region is perhaps the most diverse of all, confirming the extent to which neighbouring cultures have influenced this land in the past. That same influence continues today, making this area an intriguing place to visit.

Notes
1 Darke, Diana, *Guide to Aegean and Mediterranean Turkey*, London, 1987, p. 212.
2 For excellent charts of these waters, see: Heikell, R., *Turkish Water Pilot*, London, 1987.
3 Studies on this church are now being carried out by Ohio State University, in Columbus, Ohio, under the leadership of Prof. James Morganstern.
4 Alfoldi-Rosenheim, Elizabeth, *The Necropolis of Anemurium*, Ankara, 1971, pp. 90–92.

CHAPTER IV
SOUTH EASTERN TURKEY

The south eastern border of Turkey, which extends from Antalya on the west to Hakkari on the east, delineates the northern extent of Syria and Iraq in the process, and is almost equally as long as the Mediterranean coastline that precedes it. Through it flow the Tigris (Digle) and Euphrates (Firat) rivers which begin their long journey to the Arabian Gulf near Elaziğ in central Anatolia at the base of the Munzur mountains (plate 58). This was originally northern Mesopotamia and the beginning of the Fertile Crescent, which, along with the Nile River Valley, was the first testing ground for agriculture on a grand scale. The riverine civilisations that arose in both areas were each a result of the organisational skills primarily made necessary by the shift from a nomadic to a farming society. Names of the cities here, such as Kargamus, or Carcamesh, near the Firat, and Harran tell the story, even though the fertility of the area and the intricate irrigation system that made farming possible, have long since disappeared. Many cities here, like Urfa, Mardin, Diyarbakır and Hakkari, still have a timeless aspect to them. In Genesis, it also says: "The Lord had said to Abram, 'Leave your country your people and your father's household and go to the land I will show you. I will make you into a great nation and I will bless you. I will make your name great, and you will be a blessing. I will bless those who bless you, and whoever curses you I will curse, and all the peoples on earth will be blessed through you'. So Abram left, as the Lord had told him, and Lot went with him. Abram was seventy-five years old when he set out from Harran."[1] Harran today still looks like a place that would be easy to leave, with its beehive shaped mudbrick houses offering the only visual relief from the ever present mud flats around them (plate 59). Like the Nubians in Egypt, the people of Harran have worked out a way in which to roof over a house in mudbrick without using form-work of any kind, because of the total absence of any wood to build it. While the Nubians primarily use a vault system that leans against a vertical wall for support, the houses in Harran use a corbelled dome to roof over the main room in the house in a way that is similar to that used in many villages in Syria to the south.[2] Unlike the Nubian villages that were wiped out by the Aswan High Dam however, those of Harran will not be covered by the Atatürk Dam now being built north of Urfa, whose lake will cover thousands of square miles behind it.[3] This dam, which is part of an initiative called the Southeast Anatolian Project, may make this area fertile once again, although hopefully without the same cultural loss that the Nubians have suffered (plate 60).

As the town of Urfa itself shows however, cultural loss can occur in incrementally small ways as well as large ones. Many of the old buildings in the city have been demolished to make way for newer concrete boxes leaving only the Abdurrahman Mosque in the centre of the town as a reminder of past glory (plate

61). Organised around a beautiful pool that is meant to be symbolic of the rain sent by God to save Abraham from being burned at the stake by the Assyrian King Nimrod for destroying pagan idols, the Abdurrahman Mosque and Medrese is a relative newcomer in a region filled with ancient monuments (plate 62). Dating from the middle of the 18th century, the medrese has over thirty rooms for resident students that surround the pool and looks toward the three domes of the mosque and its tall minaret, which is visible throughout the town. The entire composition is linked together with an arcade of ogee arches that recall the distinctive outline of the high triple domes in the centre and visually repeat the form.

Mardin, which is nearly ninety kilometres to the east of Urfa has not suffered such radical alteration. Clinging to the side of a steep slope that faces the Syrian border and the barren desert to the south, the dual domes of the Sultan Isa Medrese seem admirably suited to this cliffside site, and to the barren hills below (plate 63). The medrese, which is Artukid in style, is a good example of both the Seljuk and Zengid influence that combine to make it such compelling architecture.[4] More indicative still is the Great Mosque of Dunaysir, now Kizeltepe, located just below Mardin, of which only the main prayer hall now remains. Built in 1200, it dates from the zenith of power of this unique Turcoman principality that controlled Hasenkeyf, Mardin, Harput, Diyarbakir and Kizeltepe between 1090 and 1234.

Innovations introduced at Dunaysir, such as the use of a visually dominant main dome which favoured the mihrab side of the prayer space, and an arcaded courtyard used to precede the entry into the enclosed interior, make this a very important formative development for later Ottoman architecture.

The great mosque at Diyarbakır, to the north of Mardin, dates from the very beginning of the Artukid period, having been begun by Sultan Malikshah in 1091 and added to in subsequent building programs later (plate 64). As such, it is the first Turkish mosque in Anatolia.[5] This same sultan is known to also have rebuilt parts of the Umayyad Mosque in Damascus, and the parallels between the two buildings become obvious when they are compared (figure 19). While the general dimensions of the Umayyad mosque were originally determined by the size of the foundations of the Roman Temple of Jupiter which had preceded it, and upon which it was built, there was no such regimented arrangement of the courtyard, which avoids the repetitive arcade of the Syrian model and organises buildings of various shapes and functions around an enlarged parallelogram of open space (figure 20).

Because of its lack of a dome, the Great Mosque of Diyarbakir has not had the impact upon later architecture that Dunaysir did. Because subsequent grouping of religious buildings quite like those at Diyarbakir do not exist in Anatolia, it remains both an atypical and controversial building although an undeniably engaging one. The spontaneous addition of the Zuiciriye Medrese, which closed off the south western side of the courtyard in 1199, to be followed by the Mesudiye Medrese and the Safiiler Mosque on the northern side in 1223, and the splayed arcade that closes off the eastern side along with the steeped pitched cover over the ablution fountain soon after, all give this complex great architectural interest. As Professor Doğan Kuban has said: "In south eastern Anatolia, which is geographically connected with Mesopotamia and Northern Syria, there is a stone building tradition which stretches from the mountainous regions of eastern Anatolia to Cappadocia. Based on the architecture of the late Roman period in Asia Minor and Syria, it was also influenced by the late Sassanian and Islamic traditions.".[6]

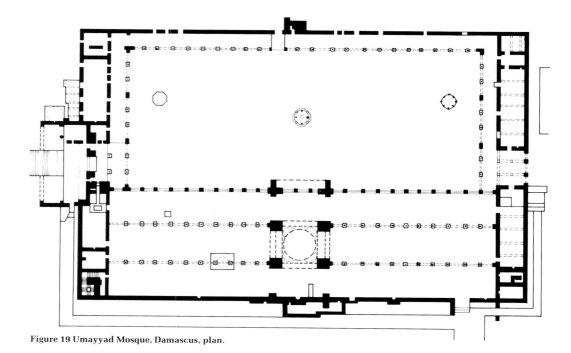

Figure 19 Umayyad Mosque, Damascus, plan.

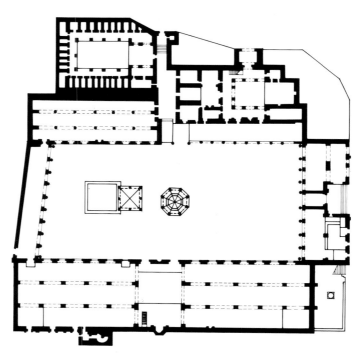

Figure 20 Great Mosque, Diyarbakir, plan.

As can be determined by its name, which means "the city of Bakr", Diyarbakir, which was settled by the Beni Bakr tribe, has had a strong Arab influence in the past, having been conquered by them in 639 AD. This influence, combined with that of a large Kurdish population, continues to give the city a highly unusual character, as do its walls, which are still virtually intact. Beginning at the citadel, which is near the banks of the Tigris, these walls cast a nearly six kilometre long circle of stone around the old part of the city, now broken only by several new highways that connect Diyarbakir with Mardin and Urfa. Having been rebuilt by Malikshah at the same time as he began construction of the Great Mosque, they were originally constructed by the Romans in 297 AD and are a marvel of military architecture. Built of three separate layers of huge black basalt blocks, they are guarded by over seventy projecting tunnels the strongest of which were located near the Roman gate of Bab al-Rumi, leading to Urfa, the great Bastion, or Ulu Badan, to Mardin, the Yeni Capi, or New Gate, facing the Tigris river, and the Harput Gate, also known as the Bab al-Armen or Gate of the Armenians, which opens up to Elazığ.

The site of Nemrut Dağ, a monument of an entirely different type and another historical period, is located ninety kilometres north of Urfa near the town of Kahta, east of Adiyaman. Because the hierothesion, or memorial tomb, is located at the top of one of the highest mountains in the region, it is still only accessible between May and October, after the snow has melted, but at least now there are roads that go there, and the journey need not be made by foot or pack animal as it had to in the past. Antiochos of Kommagene, the ruler of a dynasty who modestly claimed descent from Darius the Great of Persia (through his father Mithradates) and Alexander the Great (through his mother Laodike.[7] On the north east and south west sides of this great tumulus, directly at its base, two huge terraces have been cut into the rock face of the mountain top as a base for sculpture groupings depicting deities with which the Kommagene dynasty identified, and which were an amalgamation of Eastern and Western religious pantheons in the true Hellenistic manner. In sequence the order of both of the groupings, when seen from the front is (1) Apollo/Mithra/Helios/Hermes (2) Tyche (3) Zeus/Ahuramazda (4) King Antiochos (5) Herakles/Antagnes/Ares.[8] In addition, this grouping was flanked on each end by the eagle and the lion, the symbols of royalty. The only difference between the two groupings is that the north east terrace, which faces the dawn, also includes an elaborate stepped altar, which was probably intended for sacrifices to be made at the rising of the sun. The heads of all of the statues have since toppled to the ground, and have been set upright in positions relatively close to those they held on the terrace above (plate 65). The tomb of Antiochos Kommagene is felt to be buried beneath the stone tumulus itself, but various attempts to tunnel into the centre have caused collapses that have threatened the entire monument. Seismic profiles and vertical electric soundings have also been made by archaeologists investigating the monument, but have yet to determine what, if anything, lies in the centre of the rockhill. In the interest of preserving what has now become one of the most important sites in southeastern Turkey, further exploration has been halted.

While originally written about a monument in Egypt, Shelley's poem *Ozymandias* seems to be related more to Nemrut Dağ:

I met a traveller from an antique land
Who said: Two vast and trunkless legs of stone
Stand in the desert. Near them on the sand,
Half sunk, a shattered visage lies, whose frown,
and wrinkled lip, and sneer of cold command,
Tell that its sculptor well those passions read
which yet survive, stamped on these lifeless things,
The hand that mocked them and the heart that fed:
And on the pedestal these words appear:
'My name is Ozymandias, King of Kings:
Look on my works, ye Mighty, and despair!'
Nothing beside remains. Round the decay
Of that colossal wreck, boundless and bare
The lone and level sands stretch far away.
(plate 66).

Aside from providing a new and unprecedented lesson in the seemingly limitless reaches of the human ego, Nemrut Dağ also offers a clear example of the real legacy of Alexander the Great and the Hellenistic age that he initiated. The dates of Antiochos, from 62 to 32 BC fall nearly 300 years after Alexander's first entry into Asia Minor, prior to which religion seemed to be a much simpler affair. The pantheon of Greek gods, for one thing, had by that time been set, after several late entries. Local sects in Asia Minor and further east, which recognized totally different, and equally pantheistic deities, also had been firmly established by this time, as had those in Egypt. In Alexander, however, the Greeks discovered a king who not only started to change all that but who also embodied many of the qualities that the people had decided should belong to their gods, blurring perceptions of what the differences between the two should be. In a famous journey into the western desert made after having been crowned Pharaoh of Egypt, Alexander fulfilled a personal fantasy and visited the temple of a hyphenated deity named Zeus-Ammon who supposedly combined all of the characteristics of the father of both the Greek and Egyptian gods. As one of the several highly visible publicity moves that Alexander made to dramatise his wish to unite east and west under his leadership, this "secret" pilgrimage had the desired effect, and also started a trend. Foreign gods, especially those with attributes even remotely similar to their opposite number in the Greek pantheon, became very fashionable. More important, Alexander also made it seem acceptable, and even necessary, to deify royalty and after him this practice increased, especially among the Romans, who were very impressed with his style. Nemrut Dağ, then, represents the final synthesis of these trends; the blending of east and west that began in the Hellenistic age taken to its ultimate extreme.

Hasenkeyf, which lies over two hundred kilometres from Nemrut Dağ, near Diyarbakir, sits on a high escarpment above the Tigris looking out over the plain below. Called Cephe during the Byzantine period, its name was changed to Hasn-Cephe, or Fortress Cephe, when the Arabs invaded south eastern Anatolia. Like Mardin and Diyarbakir nearby, Hasenkeyf also shows the stamp of Artukid influence and was their capital city for some time. Having suffered greatly from the

Mongol invasions, much of the old town is in ruins, but the main gateway to the Artukid City is still standing even though the walls it led through have long since vanished (plate 67). Through this gate, a road leads up the side of the escarpment, eventually coming upon the extensive remains of the city top, which include a palace, a mosque, and many houses. On the way out of the city a domed tomb can be seen on the opposite bank of the Tigris, with glittering turquoise blue faience tiles shining in the sunlight (plate 68). This tomb, or *turbe*, which is nearly twenty-five metres high, was built for Zeynel-Bey, the son of Uzun Hasan of the Akköyunlü dynasty sometime before his death in 1473. As was typical of many of these early, free-standing tombs, the crypt in which the body was placed is located beneath the *turbe* itself, within the raised platform that acts as its base. Above this, a round domed space, accessible here by two separate stairways that have since disappeared, serve as a commemorative area, also used for prayer. Although frowned upon in orthodox Islam, *turbe* of this sort were an enduring tradition among the Turkic tribes that moved into Anatolia from the east and continued to develop as an architectural form throughout the Ottoman period, becoming more and more intricate and highly decorated in the process. There has been some supposition that the form of the *turbe* and the *kumbet* derives from the nomadic yurt, or tent, which the Turks used on their migration westward into Anatolia from Central Asia. As simply a more permanent tent, the *turbe* and *kumbet* (tomb tower) thus served as more durable final homes for the deceased, and offered a way to commemorate a single life in the midst of the wilderness through which it had come.

Notes

1 Holy Bible, New International version, New Brunswick, N. J., 1970, Genesis 12:4, p. 7.
2 Darke, Diana, *Guide to Eastern Turkey and the Black Sea Coast*, London, 1987, p. 195.
3 Ibid., p. 193.
4 Ibid., p. 210.
5 Sözen, Metin, *The Evaluation of Turkish Art and Architecture*, Istanbul, 1987, p. 34.
6 Kuhan, Doğan, *Turkish Culture and the Arts*, Istanbul, 1986, p. 30.
7 Akurgal, Ekrem, *Ancient Civilizations and Ruins of Turkey*, Istanbul, 1985, p. 348.
8 Ibid., p. 351.

CHAPTER V
THE EAST

The eastern region of Turkey, just like the south east, has been greatly influenced by the countries that border it. With Iran lining its southern half and Russia on its north, this entire area has been described as "a perennial passageway for armies and whole peoples from East to West [that] could not but affect its human, ethnic and even physical character"[1] (plate 69). As a funnel of both trade and invasions, the eastern region, perhaps more than any other, has been witness to the transfer of entire nations. One of the most critical of these took place in a village that was called Manzikert, now Malazgirt, on 19 August, 1071, northwest of Lake Van. The Byzantine emperor at this time, Romanus Diogenes, who had despaired of the constant Turkish attacks on his eastern frontier, had decided on corrective action, and had assembled a mixed force of Slavs, Turks, Franks, Sicilians and others, in addition to his own troops, with which to meet the Turkish commander Alp Aslan. As a result of Turkish defections from his army to the other side, as well as other difficulties, Romanus Diogenes was defeated and taken prisoner, thus opening up the whole of Anatolia to the Seljuk advance and their establishment of a capital at Konya in the heart of the country. After this giant breach in the Byzantine dam, which most certainly would have collapsed at some other time had it not done so in 1071, the path was opened for many Turkish tribes from Central Asia to enter Anatolia. As nomadic tribes living at subsistence level and constantly on the move to survive, these tribes looked longingly at the fertile lands to the west as a more secure and permanent homeland, and this was their chance to take it. The roll call of these tribes who came into Anatolia along with the Seljuks, or after their destruction by Mongol armies at Kose Dağ in 1243, included the Karamanids, Hamidoghullari, Eshnefoghullari, Suruhanids, Dhulgadnids, Kamazanoğhüllari and finally the Osmanli, or Ottomans who eventually came to dominate them all (plate 70).

Physically, eastern Turkey, and especially the area around Lake Van, is the visual equivalent of the music of Alexander Borodine, severe yet magnificent. Beginning at the southern most corner of the region, near Hakkari, both the Cilo and Sat mountain ranges serve as a dramatic reminder that more than sixty per cent of this nation has an altitude in excess of 750 metres above sea level, reaching its highest point of 5,137 metres at Ağri Dağ, or Mt Ararat, near the Russian border, where the remains of Noah's Ark and even Noah himself may still rest. The height and extent of all of these mountain ranges have had an enormous impact on the entire country, affecting communication, transport and weather conditions and therefore the economy as well. In eastern Anatolia in particular, the Cilo and Sat ranges continually prevent the ameliorating effects of both the Mediterranean climate and the warm, dry desert air, coming from Syria and Iraq further east, from penetrating inland. Therefore, the average precipitation levels of 750 to 2500mm a year that are common in the Mediterranean region diminish to 300 to 500mm a year in the east.[2] Because of the height and variety of the ranges here, mountain climbing is a popular sport in Turkey, but can be particularly risky near the Russian border where special permission is required. An added bonus to mountain climbing in this area is the large number of petroglyphs that can also be found here. The Gevaruk Valley in south eastern Turkey and the Tirisin Plateau have the most extensive collection of petroglyphs to be found anywhere, and the relative inaccessibility of these rock carvings has insured their preservation. The Tirisin, or Green Arrow, plateau extends eastward from the Cilo mountains, and it, along with the glacier fields of the Sat range and the Gevaruk valley between, provide a beautiful area for exploration. The first reports of petroglyphs here came from a climber named Halil Özdündar in 1937, and these have steadily increased, as more climbers go into this area.[3]

Lake Van, which covers 450 square miles, is the largest lake in Turkey and a very welcome visual oasis in this arid area. Due to the high sulphur content of the springs that feed the lake, however, the water is highly saline and not really suitable for either irrigation or swimming. Regardless of that, it is a hypnotic sight in the midst of this wasteland, alternating in colour from silver to blue-black depending on reflections from the mountains or the sun and the time of day. Such aridity has not always been the case, however, as a column discovered here in 1909 may show. Dedicated to Semiramis, whom it describes as "a woman of the palace of Samsi-Adad, King of the World, King of Assyria", confirms that the legendary beauty, like Solomon's Sheba, was quite real. Also like her Yemeni counterpart, who is known to have commissioned an extensive dam that converted a desert into a paradise, Semiramis built the Shaminarmsu, or "the waters of Semiramis" which brought water down from the top of Mt Varak to the plains of Van. These plains were once the centre of the Kingdom of Urartu which flourished here between 900 and 600 BC, and the crumpled ruin of the citadel of its capital Tushpa, which was built by King Sarduri in 840 BC, can still be seen in the hills above it. The Armenians also ruled here, creating a kingdom called Vaspurakan. As the backbone of the Byzantine army, the Armenians excelled as soldiers, to the extent that in periods when the empire was in great crisis, they rose into positions of military leadership and even contributed several emperors, such as Heraclius, to the throne.[4] They also excelled as architects and stone masons, and, due to geographic as well as religious connections with Syria, were very much influenced by the architecture there (plate 71). As Cyril Mango has said: "Armenian architecture developed at the very time when Christian Syrian architecture came to a halt; at a time, moreover, when the Byzantine empire was entering its Dark Age. It may be said without exaggeration that in the seventh century Armenian architecture was leading the entire Christian East."[5] The Church of the Holy Cross, which was built on Akhtamar Island in the middle of Lake Van nearly 300 years after the period that Mango mentions, displays the same characteristic richness of form and materials (figure 21). Friezes taken from popular Biblical stories enliven the exterior of the church, showing Jonah and the Whale, David and Goliath, Adam and Eve, Daniel in the Lions' Den, Abraham and Isaac and Samson and Delilah, all rendered in a very free, almost childlike way (plate 72).

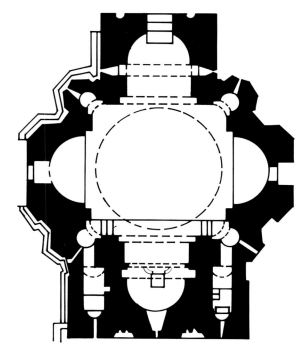

Figure 21 Akhtamar, plan.

On the same shore, near Gevaş, where the boats leave for Akhtamar, there is a *kumbet* called Halime Khatun, that dates from 1358 (plate 73). Built of the greenish-brown sandstone that is typical in this area, this twelve-sided burial structure was built for a Bey of the Karaköyunlü tribe called Abd al-Malik Izz al-Din, and is decorated with very finely carved calligraphic mouldings at its cornice as well as long thin ridges crowned with conch-shell caps, and intricate braid work belts running round the entire circumference (plate 74). This *kumbet* vaguely resembles the Bayindir mausoleum in Ahlat near Van which was a very important Seljuk stronghold in the past, but has long since been deserted (plate 75). Built by Emir Bayindir in 1492, near a mosque in his name, the *kumbet* is unusual in its use of open sides that are structured with stout columns carrying a delicate cornice. There is also a Seljuk cemetery nearby that is full of tall, intricately carved headstones recalling the strong influence that this dynasty had here in the past.

North east of Lake Van, near the Russian border, a small town called Doğubayazit is the improbable location of one of the most bizarre architectural extravaganzas imaginable. Called the Ishak Paşa Palace, the folly was built in the latter part of the 18th Century by a Bey of the Cildioglu family who was appointed a vizier here by the Ottomans in 1789, and named governor of Çildir and Ahiska. His prominence was short lived, however, and for his excesses, of which this palace is undoubtedly a prime example, he was dismissed and exiled to Hasenkale where he later died.[6] Covering a vast, 7600 square metre rectangle that projects out over a steep from one side, it is entered through an enormous portal decorated in the Seljuk manner. A *haramlik*, or harem for women, as well as a *selamlik*, or men's quarters, a mosque and servants quarters are all distributed around a secondary courtyard located behind the primary entrance enclosure, in a progression series slightly reminiscent of the Topkapı Palace in Istanbul. In addition, a throne room, reception hall and other spaces connected with the official office of the pasha, are included in the *selamlik* area. Having taken the brunt of the various military campaigns that have gone on in this area, as well as being open to the elements, the palace looks much older than it actually is, but its eclectic combination of architectural styles eventually gives it away as having been strongly influenced by the same re-examination of historical forms that was taking place in Istanbul at the end of the 18th century. Regardless of stylistic influences, the Ishak Paşa Palace remains one of a rare group of highly personal architectural fantasies that actually get built.[7]

Kars, which is north of Doğubayazit, and near the Russian border as well, once again reflects the strong ethnic influence of the Caucasus upon this region, as well as its role as one of the main gateways for westward movement into Anatolia. The Seljuk presence here is most vividly reflected in the numerous caravanserais that sprang up along the roads that stretch from Denizli to Erzerum, Kars and Igdir, as well as from Kuthaya to Malatya, Bitlis and Ahlat and from Antalya to Samsun on the Black Sea coast. These caravanserais, which one historian has labelled "service organisations", bear mute witness to the greatness of the Seljuk sultanate and the solidity of its organisation.[8] Also called *ribats*, or *hans*, these buildings basically combined all of the facilities needed by travellers of these times together into one protected unit. One such han is located at Izdir, between Doğubayazit and Kars with divisions into a double-gated, secure forecourt and rear, three aisled hall shared by men and animals alike, that was typical of these stopping places.

One of the main attractions of Kars is a visit to the village of Ani, which is very close by. Because this deserted town is in a neutral zone between the Turkish and Russian borders, entrance to it must be cleared by the Turkish military authorities. While this process is a bit time consuming, it is now simply routine. The reward for a bit of patience is a much clearer understanding of the tragedy that the Armenians who lived here, as well as most of eastern Anatolia, suffered at the hands of the Mongol invaders. Having become wealthy from the same caravans that enriched many other cities in this region in the past, Ani rose further, to rival many of the richest cities in the Middle East by the middle of the 10th century, with a population of nearly 250,000 people.[9] The cathedral of Ani, which is one of the largest remaining Armenian churches in Turkey, still stands here, having been built by the same architect that was called upon to repair the Hagia Sophia in Istanbul when its dome collapsed in 989.[10]

Erzurum lies 180 kilometres to the west of Kars, and is probably best known for the Seljuk Çifte Minare Medrese which has become a symbol for the city (plate 76). Professor Doğan Kuban has described the general role of the *medrese* by saying: "they occupied an eminent place in early Anatolian Turkish history [and] artistically were more significant than mosques. Sultans, emirs and viziers founded great madrasas in the second half of the 13th Century, the most prolific period of their artistic development. The covered madrasa eventually became a prototype for a specific mosque style in the early Ottoman period.".[11] Dating from the period that Kuban refers to, the Çifte Minare Medrese, which was built in 1253, covers an area of 60 x 90 metres (figure 22). Surrounded by a high frame, the portal, which is the predominant feature of the north side of the *medrese*, is flanked by minarets on each side which give it its name. A vestibule behind the main doorway leads to chambers on the right and left which act as structural bases for the tall minarets, and contains a mosque on the right hand side. An inner court, measuring 12 x 30 metres, is surrounded with an arcade that screens three iwans cut into the sides and back of the row of rooms hugging the high exterior wall. The iwan at the rear of the central court, on the axis with the main entry, has long since been replaced with a *kumbet*, extended out by two long flanking walls. The exuberant decoration, scale and proportion of this building make it a fine example of an open Seljuk *medrese* at its best.

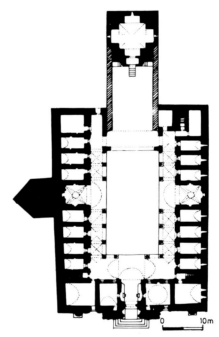

Figure 22 Erzurum Çifte Minare, plan.

The Yakutiye Medrese, which is nearby, was built soon afterwards in 1310, and its proximity to the Çifte Minare Medrese makes possible a comparison of both the covered and open *medreses* at the same time. While on the subject of the comparison of architectural types, the Mama Khatun Kumbet, which is at Tercan, halfway between Erzurum and Enzincan, offers an example of a completely different kind of burial structure to those seen at Van and Ahlat (plate 77). Considered to be one of the rarest and most important *kumbets* in Anatolia, Mama Khatun consists of a large, cylindrical structure surrounded by a deep boundary wall with niches cut into it at regular intervals around its entire circumference. This unusual design, not seen elsewhere, is felt to be a throwback to a type of tomb commonly found in Tagesken east of Lake Aral in Central Asia, adding final proof of the rich heritage of this fascinating region (plate 78).

Notes

1 Graber, O., and Hill, *The Formation of Islamic Art*, New Haven, 1973, p. 27.

2 Özek, H., and Zuzik, I., *Mediterranean Turkey*, Istanbul, no date, p. 8.

3 Alok, Ersin, *Anadoluda Kayaüstü Resimleri*, Istanbul, 1988, p. 70.

4 Mango, Cyril, *Byzantine Architecture*, Milan, 1978, p. 98.

5 Ibid., p. 98.

6 Darke, Diana, *Guide to Eastern Turkey and the Black Sea Coast*, London, 1987, p. 281.

7 For a thorough description of the palace, see: Sözen, Metin, *The Evolution of Turkish Art and Architecture*, Istanbul, 1987, p. 183.

8 Graber and Hill, op. cit., p. 26.

9 Darke, Diana, , op. cit., p. 289.

10 Mango, Cyril, *Byzantine Architecture*, op. cit., p. 130.

11 Kuban, Doğan, *Turkish Culture and the Arts*, Istanbul, 1986, p. 19.

CHAPTER VI
CENTRAL ANATOLIA

Speculation over the origins of the name Anatolia, which would initially seem to point to some connection with the Turkish word 'Anadolu' meaning "homeland", has instead currently drifted toward the Greek word "Anatole" meaning 'east of the Aegean', the direction of the sunrise. Yet, for the Hittites, who probably came from the southeast, such a concept had little meaning, and Anatolia to them was 'the land of the Hatti,' focusing mainly on what is today central Turkey. Surprisingly, there are direct parallels between the Hittite kingdom and that of Troy, which co-existed with it, since the fall of Priam's city to the Achaeans is felt to have left the Hittites and the interior of the country vulnerable to the invasions which finally wiped them out. The date of the Achaean attack in 1240 BC dovetails almost exactly into the disappearance of all traces of Hattusas which was the Hittite capital city, as well as with ancient Egyptian records of invasions by 'peoples of the sea' whose origins are still unknown. The result of the total collapse of both of these vital cultures was disastrous for Anatolia, marking the end of the Bronze Age and causing a Dark Age that lasted for two centuries.[1] Before their passing, however, the Hittites left an indelible mark on Anatolia and the rest of the kingdom which they ruled from it. They were an Indo-European people who first arrived on the plateau around 2000 BC, and ruled first from Kultepe, about 200 kilometres to the south east of present-day Ankara. The beginnings of their civilization is marked by the blending of their culture with that of the Hatti, who were indigenous to the region, and whom they replaced. This new, amalgamated society, which was also later augmented by a group called the Nesians, is known through evidence deciphered from Babylonian cuneiform tablets to have been so strong as to overthrow the famous Hammurabi's government there, and to have also invaded Syria and Egypt. Five temples have been uncovered at Hattusas and Alacahöyük, as well as a very sophisticated religious centre at Yazilikaya, nearby. In plan, Hattusas was divided into two sections, with a smaller, lower portion on the north side, a higher portion on the south, and a citadel in between. This citadel, known as Buyuk-kale, was an irregular oval fortress, protected by a huge castellated wall placed along the top of a cliff, with three separate levels inside that corresponded to the slope of the hill it was built on. These levels, in turn, were used to organise a series of interior courtyards that became progressively smaller as the slope rose, that incrementally filtered public and private areas. In this way, a large lower court that was open to the people was used for general administrative functions, followed by a more restricted religious section in the middle, and the king's palace in the smallest and most secure level at the top.[2] Assyrian influence is evident in both the construction techniques that were used and the interiorised approach, in which spaces line up against massive and solid transition points inside the city (plate 79). The only difference is that the Hittites tended to surround their courtyard with spaces that had diverse functions rather than group similar activities together, as the Assyrians did. The Hittite temple at Yazilikaya, which honours the seemingly endless pantheon of 1000 gods adopted from the Hurrians, takes its name from the word for 'carved rock', and is a remarkable integration between man-made and natural forms (figure 23). Here a long, linear building is organised into a non-symmetrical series of spaces, and closes off the mouth of a rocky defile whose walls have been turned into two sequentially ordered sculpture galleries. The story that they tell weaves the lives of King Hattuslis ('the one from Hattusa') and King Tudhaliya IV, who had the gallery built, with those of their gods, who were depicted as being very paternalistic and loving.

Hittite influence in Anatolia was not limited to the central area alone, but spread from Kultepe, Hattusas and Alacahöyük to Arslantepe (Malatya), Asitawanda (Karatepe), Sakcha (Ghensa), Samal (Zindjerli) and Hadatu (Anslantash) in the south east, as well as Eti, Yokushyu, Ahlatlibel, Karoglan and Gavourkale further to the west. By 1200 BC, however, the Hittite domination of Anatolia, which had lasted for nearly a millennium, was at an end. Their place was taken by the Phrygians, who re-occupied Hattusas at first, and then moved their capital, which they called Mushki, to Gordion, which is halfway between Ankara and Eskişehir. These were the people ruled by the legendary King Midas, who, far from being fictitious, was recognized in the court records of King Sargon II of Assyria. Many Phrygian monuments still remain around the acropolis called Midas City near Eskişehir, mostly consisting of geometrically carved tombs (plate 80).

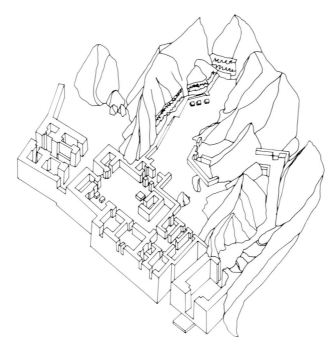

Figure 23 Yazilikaya, axonometric.

Others of the same type can be found near Afyon Karahisar, such as the monument called Arslankaya, which originally contained a statue of the goddess Cybele in the centre. The rock cliff into which it had been carved has since eroded, leaving only a sharp jagged sliver of rock still standing on the hillside (plate 81).

Cappadocia is a portion of the Hittite heartland lying to the south of Hattusas and Yazilikaya, and the cylinder seals found throughout the area prove it was heavily populated by them. Called Katpatuka by the Assyrians, which changed to Cappadocia by the time of the historian Herodotus, this province occupies a very large section of central Anatolia, from the flats of lake Tuzgölü in the west, past Malatya in the east and from Yozgut and Sivas in the north to Niğde in the south. Geothermal activity from both Mt Argaeus, now Enciyas Daği, near Kayseri, and Hasan Daği near Aksaray, first covered this entire area with a deep layer of volcanic dust millions of years ago which was then followed by a top coating of lava which cooled into harder rock. Slow erosion at weak points in the rock mantle has led to valleys of varying width having been cut into the tufa, or softer solidified ash. This has created the characteristic moonscape here, which is called *peribacileri* or 'fairy chimneys' locally (plate 82). The high potassium level of the tufa in combination with rainwater has ironically made parts of this wasteland a fertile area for growing fruit, especially grapes, apples, pears, plums and apricots, and making parts of Cappadocia some of the best wine producing areas in Turkey. Oxidation of the minerals in the tufa also creates an ever-changing spectrum of colours in each area, from the reds of Ürgüp to the pale blues of Ihara and and the rich creams of Göreme (plate 83).

Kayseri, or ancient Caesarea, which was the nearest city to the majority of these valleys in classical times, was an important Christian outpost in Central Anatolia because of its position on the trade routes from the south and the east. The commercial activity here attracted Greeks, who were in turn supplanted by Arabs during the Islamic invasion in the 7th century. Armenians fleeing the Seljuk move from the east added another ethnic layer in the eleventh century followed by Turks, Mongols and then Turks again who finally established control over the city in the mid 14th century, never to lose it again. The final upheavals in Caesarea were devastating for the Christian community there, and an exodus, similar to that caused by the Latin occupation of Constantinople, began to move east into these barren valleys for protection.

Seeing isolation here as the only safe alternative in an uncertain time when solitary akritoi, who were the Byzantine equivalent of Turkish ghazi warrior knights, were the only law in this frontier region. A monastic movement begun by St Basil of Caesarea in the 4th century gradually started to increase by the 7th and became a flood three hundred years later. In contrast to the strictly separated coenobitical units seen in the south east and elsewhere, the monastic communities set up in Cappadocia centred around the Lavra system which originated in Palestine and did not require constant, self-sufficient separation from society, but allowed mixing with the secular world.[3] For this reason, the monasteries of Cappadocia usually existed side by side with nearby villages, and were much smaller than those seen at Alahan, Anavarza, Sion and Sumela because they had no sleeping facilities. The small scale of each unit was also in keeping with St Basil's original belief that a good monastery should have no more than twenty monks. As

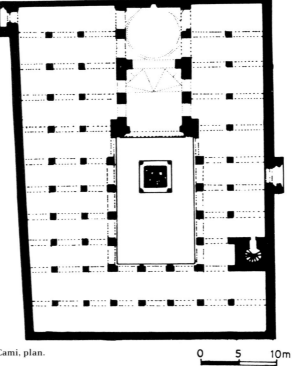

Figure 24 Malatya, Ulu Cami, plan.

0   5   10m

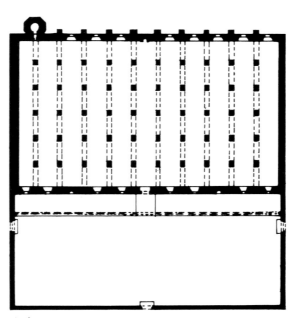

Figure 25 Sivas, Ulu Cami, plan.

Spiro Kostof has said, "despite the lack of large corporate organisation, or is it really because of it, monasteries were central to the life of the secular society. In an area where isolation from the influence of the capital was acute and danger from the outside a constant threat, the villages and small towns looked to the monk, imitator of Christ and the embodiment in theory at least of selflessness, for pre-eminent leadership in all aspects of their difficult existence."[4]

The four main areas of monastic activity which have been studied in Cappadocia to date are Göreme, Soğanlı Dere, Açık Saray and Ihlahan, or Peristrema. Göreme, and the network of valleys near Ortahisar, Üçhisar and Zilve, were the centres of Christian activity here, containing hundreds of small churches between them. Many of these, such as the Apple Church (Elmali Kil) and the Dark Church (Karanlik) are decorated with beautiful frescos, made from the vivid colours of the local pigments (plate 84). Soğanlı Dere, like Ihlahan, is a deep gorge, but differs in that it is surrounded by a natural wall of tufa, and has a wider valley floor and sides that are not as steep as Peristrema. Because it is far from the main centre of tourist activity at Göreme, Soğanlı Dere is still relatively pristine and undiscovered, making it far less commercialised. Of the more than fifty churches here, one of the most intriguing is the Yilanikilise or Snake Church, named from frescos in the interior showing women, supposedly representing the progeny of Eve, wearing real boas instead of feather ones. While their faces have been chipped away, the bodies and the snakes remain. Soganli Dere is also close to the underground troglodyte cities of Derinkuyu, which means "deep well", which held more than 20,000 people at one time and was connected to its sister city Kaymakli with a tunnel that was over 9 kilometres long (plate 85). These underground cities offered nearly complete safety and comfort to all those living there, and were virtually undetectable. Smoke from cooking fires as well as openings for ventilation were carefully hidden, and if an invader did happen to stumble upon one of the openings to the tunnels, it was sealed by a massive stone disk that rolled in grooves cut into the rock. Both cities have been empty since 1965 when the Turkish government opened them as museums.

Açık Saray, which is the third monastic centre in Cappadocia, was not as extensive as the others, with its main claim to fame being a rock-cut church that is not made out of tufa, which made its intricate designs even more difficult to do. The Ihlara Gorge, once known as Peristrema, is the fourth and last of this group and is located about seventy kilometres west of Soğanlı Dere close to Hasan Daği. Created by the Melendis River, this valley stretches from just below Selime on the north through Yaprakhisar and Belisirma to Ihlara on south, covering nearly six kilometres in its course. While not long ago this was totally uncharted territory, the churches in this valley are today dutifully marked with signs which call out strange names such as the Church of the Black Collar, or the Fragrant Church or the Church of the Crooked Stone. Yet, the atmosphere here is still primitive compared to other parts of Cappadocia, and the long walk along the river still has a feeling of high adventure.

The best base for a visit to Cappadocia may be Ürgüp, about 20 kilometres north of Nevşehir, near the centre of all the activity. Accommodation for the extended stay necessary to see this entire region properly ranges from the Club Med affiliated Kaya hotel, which is cut into the side of a rockwall, through to the more

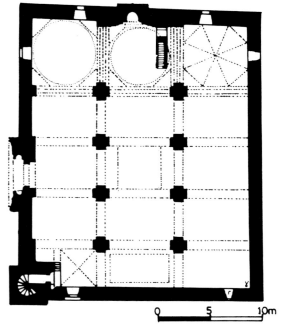

Figure 26 Nigde, Alaeddin Mosque, plan.

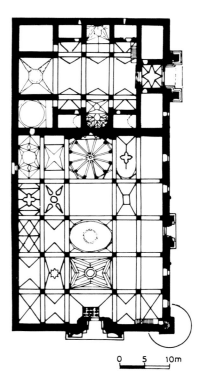

Figure 27 Divriği, plan.

conventional Turban and Buyuk Hotels nearby.

While Cappadocia may be the heart of Central Anatolia, its soul is still Turkish, and the monumental record of their triumphant march west is clearly written on the skylines of cities like Elaziğ, Malatya, Sivas, Konya, Afyon, Eskisehi and Kuthaya (plates 86, 87).

The Great Mosque of Malatya was built in 1247 by Sihabettin Ilyas Bey during the reign of the Seljuk Sultan Keykăvus II, which makes it one of the oldest in Turkey (plate 88). The plan of the building is unusual, with a central courtyard surrounded by a deep arcade and the prayer area to the south (figure 24). There is a large iwan in this mosque near the courtyard, which works in conjunction with the main dome that covers the main space in front of the *mihrab*. This spatial treatment is unique in a Seljuk mosque, making this the only one with an iwan in Anatolia.[5] The brick decoration of the mosque is exquisite, with black, green, blue and white glazed tiles working together to great effect. The Seljuk hand is also visible in the Great Mosque of Sivas, built by Qizil Arslan in 1197 during the reign of Qutb al-din Malikshah. The sheer size of the mosque is overwhelming at first, as is its hypostyle interior, with aisles perpendicular to the *qibla* (figure 25). The plainness of the exterior walls, which is broken only by the large minaret on the *qibla* wall, adds to this feeling of monumentality.[6] Sivas is also the home of the Gök, or Sky Medrese, which takes its name from the sky blue tiles on its surface. With a plan and elevation based on the repetitive use of the square, the Gök Medrese uses the classic four iwan plan now rarely extant elsewhere. In an arrangement similar to that of Çifte Minare Medrese in Erzurum, in Eastern Anatolia; the Gök Medrese uses an open central courtyard surrounded by seven bayed arcades on each side. The iwans are placed behind each of the wider arched bays in the middle of each side.

The Alaeddin Mosque in Niğde continues the string of important Islamic monuments on the way west, having been completed in 1224 by Zeyneddin Besere, who was then the governor of the province. The interior of this building is extremely compact, being divided into three aisles by two ranks of sturdy columns (figure 26). There are three domes placed side by side along the mihrab wall, with the one over the mihrab itself decorated by stalactite squinches to express its exalted central position. In true Seljuk fashion, the main portal of this mosque is its main external feature working in visual conjunction with a large cylindrical minaret at its side. Sivas boasts one of the most intricately detailed exterior portals of all (plate 89), as well as being one of the first steps toward the formation of the Külliye that were so important in Ottoman social structure later on. Completed in 1229, during the reign of Seljuk Sultan Aleddin Keykubad I whose name is recognized in the Niğde Mosque, the Divriği complex combines a prayer hall with a *darußşifa*, or hospital, which is attached to its *mihrab* wall (figure 27, plate 90).

Konya, which was the capital of the Seljuk state, is Central Anatolia's most holy Islamic city. As the centre of the Sultanate of Rum, Konya reached the peak of its power in the 13th century at the time of the famous mystic, Jalal Addin Rumi, and the Alaeddin Mosque as well as the Karatey and Ince Minare Medreses still convey the full extent of Seljuk influence.

The Alaeddin Mosque is a rather complicated building due to its having been built incrementally between 1116 and 1237 (figure 28). The mosque itself, which has a dome above it, forms the fulcrum of the composition, to which two tombs, on

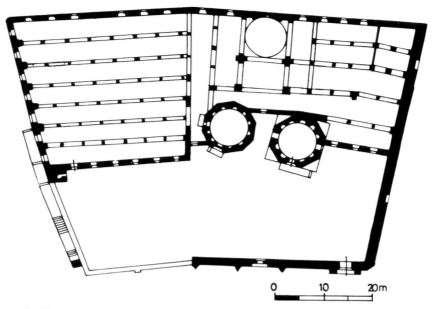

Figure 28 Alaeddin Mosque, Konya, plan.

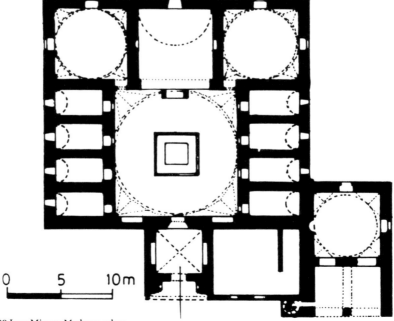

Figure 29 Ince Minare Medrese, plan.

the apron of the courtyard, were later added in a way that is characteristic of Seljuk architecture in Anatolia. The strategic location of the complex, at one of the highest places in Konya, gives the building the appearance of a citadel, and makes it a major landmark in the city.

The Karatay Medrese is opposite the Alaeddin Mosque, near the base of the same hill and is another good example of the covered type of religious school. Built in 1251, the Medrese has a particularly fine portal, which interweaves grey and white marble together in a complex of black and white tiles.

The Ince Minare Medrese, built seven later is named from the thin minaret that seems to stand over the main doorway (figure 29). Like the Karatey Medrese, it is also covered, and uses a central courtyard to organise the classrooms, and an open iwan that surrounds it. The portal of this building, unlike the others of the Seljuk period, uses interlocking calligraphy to a great extent, which makes it unique.

No trip to Konya, of course, would be complete without a visit to the Tekke of Mevlana, which is the ancient monastery of the whirling dervishes. The Tekke, which is named after the founder of the order, Mevlana Jalal Addin Rumi, is easily recognized by the green tiled conical tower which is a landmark in the city today.

The Mosque of Eşrefoğlu, at the end of this journey, shows the great variety that was possible within the crafts system of this early period. Near the lake in Beyşehir this mosque capitalises on the use of wood as the prevalent local material, in a way that brings out its essential qualities. As one of a series of 'forest mosques', the entrance gate here uses a technique called *kundekari*, in which the wooden pieces are put together like a puzzle, without the use of any nails (plate 91). This adaptation to local circumstances, which is so characteristic of Seljuk creativity, shows why these initial, tentative steps first taken in Central Anatolia later formed the basis for future achievements in Istanbul and elsewhere.

Notes
1 Akurgal, Ekrem, *Ancient Civilizations and Ruins of Turkey*, Istanbul, 1985, p. 12.
2 See: Bittel, Kurt, *Hattusha: the Capital of the Hittites*, New York, 1970, for a complete analysis.
3 Kostof, Spiro, *Caves of God*, Cambridge, 1978, p. 52.
4 Ibid., p. 56.
5 Sözen, Metin, *The Evolution of Turkish Art and Architecture*, Istanbul, 1987, p. 46.
6 Ibid., p. 42.

CHAPTER VII
THE BLACK SEA COAST

In the last part of the 13th century, the autonomous Byzantine state shattered into pieces, primarily as a result of the Latin occupation that had been forced upon it after the conquest of Constantinople in 1204 by a combined Venetian and Crusader force. Five foreign emperors in succession on the Byzantine throne between 1204 and 1261 consolidated this process, leaving various principalities scattered throughout the empire. One of the most powerful of these was the 'Empire of Trebizond' on the coast of the Black Sea near the present USSR border. This 'empire' was ruled by the Comnenus family, who themselves had intermittently seen family members in power in Byzantium since the rule of Issac I Comnenus in 1057. The Comneni turned Trebizond (which was named from the Greek word for table) into an impregnable fortress, encircling the long high plateau with walls that looked down into deep valleys on each side, and placing their palace at the most strategic point. The effective natural defences had previously allowed the city to turn away Seljuk assaults during their movement west, and combined with its commanding position at a junction of trade routes from both land and sea had helped to ensure the city's continued growth. Alexios and David Comnenus, who were the grandsons of the Byzantine Emperor Alexios I, took over the city within a month after Constantinople fell to the Fourth Crusade, and began a renaissance of church building there that outlasted the Ottoman takeover of the capital in 1452 by almost a decade.

One of the most well known results of this creative period is the Church of the Hagia Sophia in Trebizond, which best shows the city's role as an ethnic melting pot (figure 30). Built by the Emperor Manuel I, the church appears today much as it did when it was first opened in 1238, not having been significantly altered since.[1] As a melange of Arab horseshoe and gothic quatrefoil arches, Seljuk inspired stone carving, an Armenian central drum, Georgian porches, and a Byzantine cross-in-square plan, the building is certainly different from other Byzantine architecture of this period. This trend towards inventiveness and electicism, which is also seen to a lesser extent in other churches throughout the city, consistently focuses on an elongated basilica plan, levitated domes set in from their drums for lightness, Armenian style barrel vaults in the aisles, exonarthax porches, single rather multiples windows, pointed arches and intricate stonework and frescos (plates 92, 93) As one scholar has noted, 'The earliest and most powerful influences were Anatolian [and] may all originally have come from the plateau, and since most of the existing Trebizond churches were probably built after the Seljuk Turks had put an end to such activity in most of Asia Minor, the tenacity of the tradition . . . is remarkable'.[2]

The churches that still exist in Trebizond, in which many of these indigenous

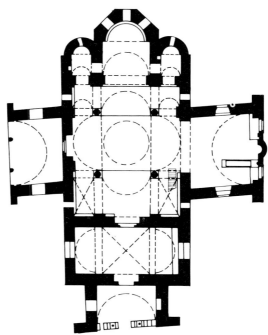

Figure 30 Hagia Sophia, Trebizond.

traits can be seen, are Panaghia Chrysocephalus (or the Virgin of the Golden Head),
St Andrew, St Eugene (which is now the Yeni Cuma Mosque) and St Philip (now
Kudreddin Cami).

In the Sumela Monastery, about fifty kilometres from Trebizond the same
monastic initiative that has produced such dramatic architecture throughout other
parts of Anatolia has undoubtedly produced its most memorable monument.
Panaghia tou Melos, later corrupted into Sumelas, was founded as a safe refuge for
an icon called the Virgin of the Black Rock, painted by St Luke. The monastery,
which seems to defy gravity as it hangs on its high cliff in the Pontic mountains,
gained new status when Alexios III Comnenus chose it as the venue for his
coronation in 1340. This act of royal sanction, which was commemorated in frescos
in the interior, brought a new and short lived surge of notoriety and prosperity to
the order. Continuing fame, along with the exceptional circumstances of the
monastery, continued to encourage a tolerant attitude towards it after the fall of
Trebizond to the Ottomans, which eventually led to aspirations for the
establishment of a nuetral zone called Pontus to be centred around the building.
After Atatürk formed the Turkish Republic in 1923, all such hopes were finally
dashed and the monastery was abandoned. The icon called the Virgin of the Black
Rock, which had managed to remain safe here for so long has subsequently been
moved to a new Sumela in Greek Macedonia, leaving the vandalised shell of the old
to the tourists (plate 94).

The Black Sea coast is a land of mists, caused by the colder air coming in from
the mountains of the interior. These mountains, more specifically called the
Giresin and Karadeniz chains, are located at some distance back from the coast.

They are fairly low toward the west, but get progressively higher toward the east, forcing clouds to drop their moisture on their northern slope. The result is lush vegetation, with tea and corn, hazelnuts and different strains of tobacco (that have made Turkish cigarettes famous all over the world) being the mainstays of the economy here.

Settlers from Megarus, Miletus, Persia and even Scandinavia (according to a theory based on evidence of vernacular decorations), in addition to Turkic influence, have created a great cultural cross section in this area (plate 95). There is also a direct correlation between the distribution of population and the topography, especially in the east, with clusters on the higher plateaus, as well as on the flat coastal plains, where most settlements are located. The time honoured migration from the coast to the highlands to escape the summer heat still takes place here, which also helps in grazing the various animals which are also a mainstay of a largely agricultural economy. The heat, while never as intense as it is in other regions of Anatolia because of cloud cover, can still be considerable for people who are unaccustomed to a warm climate.[3] Due to rising population and a lack of additional arable area to support it economically, a majority of adult men have now also migrated to the major cities in the region, so that in all of the five Black Sea provinces except Samsun, women make up most of the population of the villages and towns. Women have always had a prominent role in the history of the area, as the Black Sea was also once supposedly the home of the Amazons who came from the Caucasus to settle there. A coastal village named Terme, once called Termiscyra, may have been their capital, where legend says that the men of another Caucasian tribe called the Gargareans would be summoned each year to perpetuate the Amazon race. The male children of this annual union were killed, while the girls would be trained to be members of the warrior society. Caucasian women from Trebizond were also highly prized as wives among both the Byzantines and the Ottomans, and were renowned for both their beauty and intelligence.

There is a great difference between the vernacular architecture here and the rest of Anatolia. As Professor Orhan Özgüner notes, the difference is primarily due to the compactness of villages elsewhere in Turkey as compared to the scattered houses here. As he says: 'Scattered settlement brings a different order of living and working. The strong direct physical connection between the residential area and the centre is broken. One cannot see houses near the town centre, which is so located as to serve several villages at a time. Because of this loose connection between the houses and the town centre, the open market, mosque and tea house have a special place in the social life.'[4]

The scattering of houses which is so noticeable here is primarily due to the relationship between each farmhouse and the fields that are connected with it. This fact, as well as the prevalence of water, results in greater self-sufficiency and less need for the closely knit village architecture seen elsewhere in Turkey. An abundance of wood has also led to the use of a distinctive skeletal construction being used, with a characteristic earth and plaster infill which gives the exterior of the houses a precise chequerboard pattern.

Around Trebizond, Artvin and Rize there is also a special building type called a *serander*, which is usually made up of two spaces which are organised in different ways depending on the circumstances and the desire for variety (figure 31). Both the floor and the ceiling of these units, which are usually raised off the uneven ground on stilts, are lowered to allow for cross ventilation, and they are used for both living and the storage and drying of crops.

The village of Saframbolu, on the western end of the coast near Kastamonu, is a contrasting example of a typical traditional Turkish town.

Doğan Kuban, who has been an enthusiastic promoter of Saframbolu because of its authenticity and unspoilt quality has analysed it as a living example of a rapidly disappearing part of Turkish life. He found that the ground floor (plate 96) of many of the houses is given over to the *hayat*, which creates a small zone that is divided off from the central courtyard by a perforated wooden screen. In addition, an open gallery, or *cadak*, on the first floor, runs around the entire perimeter of this open court, with an iwan added to it for sitting in the open air. Another typical characteristic of the Saframbolu houses, which they share with the typical traditional Turkish house, is the roof overhang (plate 97). Having emerged exclusively as a structural invention used with wooden construction, this overhang, or *çikma*, developed as a result of narrow, irregular streets and varied building lots, and allowed builders to change the shape and area of the upper stories of a house while adhering to the restricted street line at the ground floor.[5] Saframbolu offers a unique opportunity to see how one main vernacular tradition of Turkish domestic architecture evolved, a tradition which faces many difficulties in this respect which it shares with other parts of the world.

Şile, at the western extreme of the Black Sea, escapes the typical combination of mountains and coast that creates the cooler, wetter climate typical of most of this

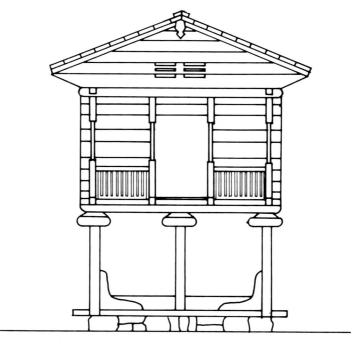

Figure 31 *Serander*, Trebizond area.

region. Because of the warmer weather and better beaches here, it has become a popular resort area for people coming from Istanbul, which is nearby. From there it is just a short trip down the coast and across the Bosphorus to the city where the story of modern day Turkey really began.

Notes

1 Mango, Cyril, *Byzantine Architecture*, Milan, 1978, pp. 141 and 166.
2 Ballance, Selina, 'The Byzantine Churches of Trebizond', *Anatolian Studies*, Ankara, 1962, p. 173.
3 Özgüner, Orhan, 'Village Architecture: Eastern Black Sea', *METU*, Ankara, 1970, p. 123.
4 Ibid., p. 123.
5 Kuhan, Doğan, *Turkish Culture and the Arts*, Istanbul, 1986, p. 35.

NOTES FOR THE TRAVELLER

Istanbul

While not the most budget conscious of choices, the Ayasofya Pansiyonlari is an ideal location from which to explore the Hagia Sophia, Topkapi Palace and other monuments nearby. It is located at 34400 Sultanahmet, Istanbul (tel. 513 36 60, telex 23841 TSAP.TR).

The Yeşil Ev, or Green Mansion, hotel is in the same league, located at Sultanahmet, tel. 528 67 64.

The Sarniç restaurant, which has been resurrected from a crumbling Byzantine cistern, is a scenic, if not culinarily inspired, place to eat. The Sarniç is located at the end of Soğukçeşme St, near the Ayasofya Pansiyon.

The Konyali Restaurant inside the grounds of the Topkapi Palace is a wonderful place to break for lunch after touring the Treasury. Located behind the Mecidiye Kiosk, it has terraces that offer a beautiful view of Istanbul and serves good *börek*, *kebap*, *shashlik* and mixed grill.

In Beyoğlu, the Pera Palas Hotel, whilst expensive, offers a unique way to experience the past glory of this part of town. It is located at the top of the hill of Meşrutiyet Caddesi 98 (tel. 151 45 60). Rejans Restaurant nearby continues a nostalgic review of 'la vie en rose'; Rejans, Olivo Gecidi 15, near Istiklal Caddesi, Galatasaray (tel. 144 16 10).

One of the two branches of Sütte delicatessen is also nearby at Dudu Odalar Sokak no. 21 (tel. 144 92 92) and a famous speciality is *basterma*, which is a type of dried meat.

Turkish food in general is vastly underrated, or even unknown, in the West, but is a great source of national pride. *Dolmalar*, or cold dishes stuffed with pine nuts, flavoured rice and currants, are excellent and include seafood (such as mussels), vine leaves, or vegetables such as egg plant and peppers. *Börek*, which are pastry triangles or rolls filled with meat, cheese or vegetables and deep fried, are also delicious. Turkish soups, or *çorba*, are also a revelation, and include fish, tomato, lentils and rice, vermicelli, barley, chicken and other wonderful varieties. A *rakı* table, based around the Turkish version of anisette, is a great national pastime, in which the drink, without water for the stout-hearted, and with for the wise, serves as a centrepiece for the *meze*, or hors d'oeuvre, that are served with it. The *meze*, which are all presented for selection, usually include *beyazpeynir* (white cheese), *yaprak dolması* (stuffed vine leaves), *pilakı* (cold white beans with tomato), *patlıcan salatası* (aubergine purée), *midye tava* (fried mussels with garlic sauce) and various kinds of fresh fruit, such as cantaloupe. the *meze* are ingeniously designed to help in blunting the effect of the *rakı*, and gradually the two work together very well. Lamb in many guises is also a national specialty, particularly *Adana kebap* or roasted *köfte* with spices, *döner kebap*, which is roasted slowly in a pit filled with charcoal, *etli pide* (flat bread covered with ground lamb) and *karışık ızgara*, or mixed grill. Other culinary treasures in this widely diverse cuisine are grilled fish (*balık*) such as bluefish (*lüfer*), swordfish (*kiliç*), sea bass (*levrek*), shrimp (*karides*), lobster (*ıstakoz*) and tuna (*palamut*). Many restaurants in Istanbul do wonders with fish, such as Liman, on Rihtim Caddesi, in Karaköy, (tel: 144-93-49) or Pandeli, near the Spice Market (tel: 522-5-34), the numerous waterside cafés in Tarabya, or the elegant Körfez, across from the Rumeli Hisarı, which runs its own boat back and forth from the shore as a shuttle. There is also an access from Körfez Caddesi (no. 78, Kanlıca) tel: 332-01-08-332-22-23. Nothing is as dear to the heart of the residents of Istanbul as having dinner with friends at a table by the water's edge, and watching the lights on the long silhouette of the opposite shore appear at dusk. Everyone has their own favourite, but two of the best of these are the Işkele in Çengelköy, or the Deniz Park in Yeniköy. Arnavutköy and Bebek also have a good selection of waterside restaurants.

Other restaurants in Istanbul that should be considered, for their good food and locations, are the Malta Köşkü in Yildiz Park (tel: 160-04-54), Sürreya on Bebek Caddesi in Arnavutköy (tel: 163-55-76) and the Hacı Bekir Oğulları Lahmacun, Kebap ve Pide Salonu, which is famous for its kebabs and is located near the Blue Mosque in Sultanahmet Square, on Torun Sokak. the dining room in the Hıdıv Kasrı, which was once the palace of the Egyptian Khedive, and is located in Çubuklu on the Asian coast, is also worth a visit.

There are several small hotels on the Princes' Islands, but the Hotel Splendid at 23 Nisan Caddesi 71, is especially evocative of an earlier, more serene age (tel: 351-67-75) Büyükada.

The dining rooms in the larger hotels in Istanbul are generally excellent, but also have prices that are much higher than restaurants outside. In spite of this, that of the Hilton Hotel on its ground floor, is extremely good, as is the food in the Divan on Cumhurriyet Caddesi.

No discussion of Turkish food would be complete without mention of *tatlılar*, or desserts, and Turkish coffee. *Baklava* is the most well known of all, of course, but there is also *kadayif*, which is like shredded wheat stuffed with nuts and soaked in syrup, and many other exotic choices, like *aşure*, and *kadın göbeği*, or 'lady's navel'. Turkish coffee (*kahve*) comes *şekerli* (heavily sugared), *orta* (medium), *az şekerli* (very little sugar) and *sade* (without).

The Aegean Coast

Assos is still an unspoilt fishing port, with a wonderful small hotel called the Behram at water's edge. It can be booked through Bursa Irtihat: Gümüşçeken Cad. no. 7 Bursa (tel: (24) 221580-215232 or 213960) or write to the director at Aycacik, Behramkale 16.

In Foça, the Club Méditerranée can be arranged through their offices at 106 Brompton Road, London SW3 (tel: 01-581 1161) or at 3 E54th St, New York, N.Y. 10022 (tel. 212 750 1687). In addition to the club in Foça, they also have installations in Kuşadase, Palmiye and Kemer. The number for the Foça club itself is 010 90 54 31 and reservations are essential.

The Çeşme Caravanserai can be arranged by writing to Çeşme Kalesi yani-Çeşme, Izmir, Turkey (tel. 9 5492/6492, telex 53868 GOLD TR [Altinyunus Group].

In Ayvalik, the Büyük Berk Hotel has one of the best locations, right in the centre of the beach, at Sarimsakli (tel. 2311). The Murat Reis, which is further away, at Küçükkoy, is also recommended (tel. 1680).

In Datça, the Club Datça Tatil Kÿü is convenient for the centre of this charming fishing village (tel. 1170).

Efes, or Ephesus, has few places to stay at the time of writing but is quickly being provided with them. The closest to the ruins at the moment is the Tusanmotel, Efes, Efesyolu 38 (tel. Selçuk 5451 60). There is also another Tusan near the ruins at Pergamon (Bergama) (tel. 1173).

The most beautiful beaches at Fethiye, Marmaris and Ölu-Deniz, are now receiving much attention from contractors wanting to build hotels near them. The best now are the Dedleoğlu in Fethiye (tel. 4010), the Marti Holiday Village in Marmaris (tel. 4910) or the Turhan Marmaris Holiday Village (tel. 1843) and the Bayaş Yünus in Ölu Deniz.

The Mediterranean

Along the Mediterranean, the Turhan Alalya Hotel in Antalya is central to all the activity in the old city and near the harbour (tel. 180 66). Many *gülets* in the yacht haven are available for hire, even though they may not advertise; enquiries are best made directly with some bargaining expected. Prices for a day trip, or overnight stays of two, three or more days, are normally so low, that bargaining is unseemly. Meals are usually provided.

The incomparable Side Palace Hotel, which is near all the ruins, and is a post-modern lesson in Turkish architectural history all on its own, can be booked through Taksim Tours Halaskarğazi Caddesi no. 34, Harbiye Sş Hani Kat 7, 80220 Harbiye, Istanbul, (tel. 132 16 06, telefax 140 17 55). Taksim Tours can be most helpful in bookings throughout Turkey.

South and East

In the south and east the Hotel Harran in Urfa is pleasant and provides a good base to see the area nearby (tel. 4918), as are the Dıyarbakir Büyük (tel. 158 32) and Turistik (tel. 126 62) in Diyarbakır.

For mountain climbing information contact the Turkish Mountaineering Club, BTGM, Ulus Işhani, A Block, Ulus, Ankara.

Central Anatolia

In central Anatolia the Museum of Anatolian Civilizations in Ankara, near the Hısar at the top of the hill, provides a good review of Turkish history, especially the more archaic civilzations.

In Cappadocia, the Kaya Hotel in Uçhısar is a good choice, as is the Büyük in Ürgüp (on Kayseri Caddesi, tel. 1060).

The Black Sea

On the Black Sea coast the Usta, on Telegrafhane Sokak 3 (tel. 121 95) in Trabzon is useful, as is the Kumhaba on the beach in Şile.

CLASSICAL PLACENAMES WITH MODERN EQUIVALENTS

CLASSICAL NAME	PRESENT NAME
Abydos	Abide
Adrianople	Edirne
Aizani	Çavdarhısar
Antioch	Antakya
Antiphellos	Kaş
Aphrodisias	Uçagız
Aspendos	Serik
Assos	Behnamkale
Atlalia	Antalya
Constantinople	Istanbul
Caesarea	Kayseri
Carcamesh	Birecik
Didyma	Didim
Edessa	Urfa
Ephesus	Efes
Gordion	Yassihöyük
Halicarnassos	Bodrum
Heraklea (of Pontus)	Ereğli
Hierapolis	Pamukkale
Iconium	Konya
Knidos	Datça
Laodikea	Denizli
Magnesia on the Meander	Ortaklar
Miletus	Söke
Mylasa	Milas
Myra	Demre
Nicea	Iznik
Nicomedia	Izmit
Olba-Diocaesarea	Uzuncaburç
Pergamon	Bergama
Perge	Aksu
Philadelphia	Alaşehir
Phoaeca	Foça
Prusa	Bursa
Sardis	Sart
Seleukia	Silifke
Smyrna	Izmir

CLASSICAL NAME	PRESENT NAME
Telmessos	Fethiye
Tralles	Aydin
Trebizond	Trabzon
Troy	Truva
Xanthos	Kinik

SELECTED BIBLIOGRAPHY

Akurgal, Ekrem, *Ancient Civilizations and Ruins of Turkey*, Istanbul, 1985.

Alfoldi-Rosenheim, Elizabeth, *The Necropolis of Anemurium*, Ankara, 1971.

Alok, Ersin, *Anadoluda Kayaüstü Resimleri*, Istanbul, 1988.

Bacon, Edmund, *Design of Cities*, New York, 1967.

Ballance, Selina, 'The Byzantine Churches of Trebizond',
    Anatolian Studies, Ankara, 1962.

Barey, Andre, 'Along the Banks of the Bosphorus', *Lotus International*, no. 26,
    Milan, 1980.

Betancourt, P. P., *The Aeolic Style in Architecture*, Princeton, 1977

Bittel, Kurt, *Hattusha: the Capital of the Hittites*, New York, 1970.

Borie, Alain, et al., 'Istanbul', *Bulletin d'Informations Architecturales*, Institut
    Français d'Architecture, Singapore, 26 Dec. 1987.

Darke, Diana, *Guide to Aegean and Mediterranean Turkey*, London, 1987.

Denny, Walter B., 'A Sixteenth Century Architectural Plan of Istanbul', *Ars
    Orientalis*, vol. VIII, 1970.

Goodwin, Godfrey, *A History of Ottoman Architecture*, London, 1971.

Graber, O., and Hill, *The Formation of Islamic Art*, New Haven, 1973.

Hanfmann, G. M., *From Croesus to Constantine*, Ann Arbor, 1975.

Heikell, R., *Turkish Water Pilot*, London, 1987.

'Istanbul: Doğasi-Tariki-Ekonomisi-Kültürü', *Yurt Ansiklopedisi*, Istanbul, 1966.

Jones, A. H. M., *The Greek City from Alexander to Justinian*, Oxford, 1984.

Kostof, Spiro, *Caves of God*, Cambridge, 1978.

Kuban, Doğan, *Turkish Culture and the Arts*, Istanbul, 1986.

Le Corbusier, *Toward a New Architecture*, Paris, 1922.

Mango, Cyril, *Byzantine Architecture*, Milan, 1978.

Özek, H., and Zuzik, I., *Mediterranean Turkey*, Istanbul, no date.

Özgüner, Orhan, 'Village Architecture: Eastern Black Sea', *METU*, Ankara, 1970.

Scully, Vincent, *The Earth, the Temple and the Gods*, New Haven, 1969.

Sumner-Boyd, H., *Strolling through Istanbul*, London, 1987.

Sözen, Metin, *The Evaluation of Turkish Art and Architecture*, Istanbul, 1987.

Wycherley, R. E., *How the Greeks Built Cities*, New York, 1969.

INDEX

Abd al-Malik Izz al-Din 140
Abdül Aziz 40
Abdül Hamid I 15, 40
Abdül Hamid II 43
Abdül Mecit 40
Abdurrahman Mosque 132, 133
Abraham 133
Academy of Athens 13
Achilles 47
Açik Saray 148
Actium 49
Adana 59
Adiyaman 135
Aeolic order 48
Aeolis 48
Aesclepion 52
Afyon 150
Afyon Karahisar 146
Alfred Agache 16
Agalar Mosque 22
Age of the Tulips 15, 35
Agri Dağ, or Mt Ararat 138
Ahiska 140
Ahlat 140, 141
Ahlatlibel 145
Ahmed III 23, 35
Ak Deniz 59
Akagalar, or the White Eunuchs'
  Gate 22
Akhtamar Island 139
Akköyunlü 137
Akritoi 146
Aksaray 146
Alacahöyük 144, 145
Alaeddin Mosque, Nigde 150
Alahan 146
Alahan monastery 130
Alanya 129
Alay Meydani 19
Aleddin Keykubad I 150
Alexander the Great 11, 47, 54, 59,

64, 129, 135, 136
Alexandria 48
Alexandria Troas 47
Alexios I 153
Alexios III Comnenus 154
Alhambra 24
Alibey Island 49
Alp Aslan 138
Alyattes 53
Amazons 55, 155
Anadolu 144
Anadoluhisari 38
Anamur 59, 129
Anavarza 130, 146
Anazarbus 130
Andys 53
Anemurium 129
Ani 141
Ankara 16, 44, 144, 145
Anslantash 145
Antalya 56, 59, 62, 129, 141
Anthemieus of Tralles 13
Anthony and Cleopatra 54
Antigonus 49
Antioch 130
Antiochos of Kommagene 135
Apasas 54
Apellikon 54
Aperlae 62
Aphrodisias 56
Aphrodite 56
Apple Church (Elmali Kil) 148
Aqueduct of Valens 12
Archaeological Park 16
Aristotle 48
Arslankaya 146
Arslantepe 145
Artemis 53
Artemisia 60
Artukids 133
Artvin 155

Arycanda 129
Arz Odasi 22
Arzhane, or Presentation Room 22
Asitawanda 145
Aspendos 64, 129
Assos 48, 61
Assyrians 145
Atatürk 16, 154
Atatürk Dam 132
Athena Polias 50
Athens 50
Atik Valide 36
Attalid kings of Pergamon 48
Attalos I 50
Attila 9
Augusteion 13
Ayasofia Pansiyonlari 24
Ayazma Cami 36
Aydin 56, 57
Ayvalik 48, 49

Bab-i Sa'adet, or Gate of Felicity 22
Baba Dag 56
Bâbüsselâm 20
Babylon 49
Bafo family of Venice 33
Baghdad Kösk 23
Bakanliklararasi Commission 16
Balat 57
Bandirma 47
Barbarossa 41
Baroque style 30
Basoda or selamlik 38
Baths of Zeus-Xeuthippes 12
Bayezit 14, 58
Bayezit II 62
Bayezit Square 27, 28
Bayindir 140
Bayindir mausoleum 140
Bedesten 33Behramkale
Belen Pass 130
Belgrade 14
Belisirma 148
Bergama 52
Besiktas 40
Besir Aga 22
Beylerbey Mosque 40
Beylerbey Palace 39
Beyoglu 43

Beysehir 152
Bin Tepe 53
Bitlis 141
Black Eunuchs 21
Bodrum 47, 56, 58, 59, 60, 61
Bosphorus Bridge 39
Bostanci 42
Brussa 44
Brutus 61
Bulbul Dagi (Mt Coressos) 55
Bursa 44
Bursa mosques 36
Büyükada 42
Byzas 9

Caesarea 146
Callicrates 51
Çanakkale 47
Çandarli 53
Cappadocia 146
Caravanserais 54, 141
Cardo maximus 12
Caria 56, 59
Cariyeler 22
Carriage Gate or Araba Kapisi 21
Cassander 49
Castle of St Peter 60
Çelik Gülersoy 24
Cellâd çesmesi, or Executioner's Fountain
  20
Celsus Library in Ephesus 12, 55
Cemil-Beyhouse 41
Cephe 136
Çesme 53, 54, 56, 61
Ceyhan 130
Chalcedon 11
Charisian Gate 12
Chinese porcelain 21
Chios 54
Christianity 55
Chrysopolis 11, 35
Church and State 13
Church of the Black Collar 148
Church of the Crooked Stone 148
Church of the Holy Apostles 12, 30
Church of the Holy Cross 139
Çifte Minare Medrese 141, 150
Cigri 47
Cildioglu family 140

Çildir 140
Cilicia 59, 129
Cilician Gates 130
Cilo mountains 139
Çinici Hasan Usta 19
Çinili Kösk 19
Cleopatra 49
Comnenus family 153
Companions of the Prophet Mohammed 32
Constantine 9, 11
Constantius Chlorus 11
Corfu 33
Corinthian capitals 58
Coronations 21
Cotton Fortress of Pamukkale 56
Covered Bazaar 33
Croesus 53
Crusades 9, 130
Cybele 53, 146
Cyprus 129

Dalyan river 61
Damascus 46
Dandolo, Enrico 9
Dardanelles 47
Darius the Great 135
Dark Church (Karanlik) 148
Datça 53, 61
Delos 57
Delphi 57
Demre 62
Denizli 141
Derinkuyu 148
Dhulgadnids 138
Didyma 56, 57
Didymaon of Apollo 57
Dimetokda 47
Diocletian 11, 12
Divan Yolu 26
Divan, or Imperial Council 20
Divrigi 150
Diyarbakir 132, 133, 135, 136
Dogubayazit 140, 141
Dolmabahçe Palace 40
Doric temple 48
Dudu Odlar Sokak 44

Eba Eyüp 32
Economic School of Marmara University
  18

Edirne 46
Edirne Capi or Edirne Gate 30
Edremit 49
Efes 56
Elazig 132, 135, 150
Eminönü 30, 33
Enciyas Dagi 146
Enderun 22
Enzincan 142
Ephesus 53, 55
Erectheum 51
Erivan 23
Erzurum 141, 150
Eshnefoghullari 138
Eskisehir 145, 150
Esmehan 24
Esrefoglu 152
Esvabi Odasi, or the Room of the Robe 24
Eti 145
Eugenie, Empress 40
Eumenes 50
Eumenes II 51
Euphrates (Firat) 132
Eve 148
Eyüp 31
Eyüp Ansari 32
Eyüp Cami 32

'fairy chimneys' 146
Fatih the Conqueror 14, 30
Fethiye 59, 61, 62
Fevzi Paşa Caddesi 30
First Crusade 130
Firuz-Bey Mosque 58
Foça, or Phocala 53, 61
Forum 12
Forum Arcadii 12
Forum Bovis 12
Forum Taurii 12
Fourth Crusade 130, 153
Fragrant Church 148
Frederick Barbarossa 130
Frescos 148

Galata 42
Galata Bridge 11, 30, 33
Galata Port 15
Galata Tower 42
Gargareans 155

Gate of the Lifegiving Spring 9
Gauls 55
Gavourkale 145
Gecis Donemi Tedbirleri 16
Gediz river 53
Genoese merchants 42
Gevaruk Valley 139
Gevas 140
Geyre 56
Ghaznavids 44
Ghensa 145
Gök, or Sky Medrese 150
Gokova Bay 60
Göksu 130
Golden Gate 12
Golden Horn 9, 30
Gonan 47
Gordion 145
Göreme 146, 148
Grand Bazaar, or Kapali arsi 26
Granicus 47
Great Mosque of Diyarbakir 133
Great Mosque of Dunaysir 133
Great Mosque of Malatya 150
Great Mosque of Sivas 150
Greater Istanbul Plan 16
Green Mosque 45
Gritti, Alvisi 43
Gritti, Andrea 43
Gület 60
Gullubache 56
Gülnus Emetullah Sultan 35
Gümüslük 60
Gusulhane 38
Gyges 53

Hadatu 145
Hadrian 55, 62
Hagia Eirene (Holy Peace) 12, 18
Hagia Sophia 12, 13, 16, 18, 26, 141
Hagia Sophia in Trebizond 153
Hakkari 132, 138
Haliç 31, 42
Halikarnassos 60
Halime Khatun 140
Hamidoghullari 138
Hammurabi 144
Haramlik 140
Harbeye 15

Harem, or women's quarters 21, 38
Harpagos 61
Harput 133, 135
Harran 132
Hasan Dagi 146
Hasankeyf 133, 136
Haseki Sultan 21
Hasenkale 140
Hatti 144
Hattusas 144
Hattuslis 145
Hayrettin Aga 26
Hellenism 59
Hellenistic Age 47
Heracleia 57
Heraclius 139
Hermias 48
Herodotus 146
Hiera 56
Hieropolis 56
Hippodrome 9, 18
Hirkai Sa'adet, or Pavilion of the Holy
  Mantle 22
Hisarlik 47
Hittites 144
Hoca Firuz-Bey 58
Hurrians 145
Hürriyet Meydani 26
Hussein Effendi 32
Hyderpasha Port 15

Ibrahim 23
Ictinus 51
Iftariye, or Feast of Ramadan Pavilion 23
Igdir 141
Ihara 146
Ihlara Gorge 148
Ilyas Bey Mosque near Miletus 57
Ince Minare Medrese 152
Incirlik, or Fig Park 23
Industrial Revolution 46
Ionic order 48
Ipsus 49
Isadorus of Miletus 13
Isfahan 24
Ishak Paşa Palace 140
Issac I Comnenus 153
Istanbul Archaeological Museum 11
Istanbul Museum 48

Istanbul Museum of Archaeology 20
Istanbul University 26
Istiklâl Caddesi 43
Izmir 53, 54
Iznik tiles 24, 34

Jalal Addin Rumi 150
Janissary corps 15, 19, 29
Jerid field 20
Jerusalem 130
Jewish community 53
Julius Caesar 56, 129
Justinian 17, 26

Kadiköy 14, 42
Kadirli 131
Kahisa Kadin or Head Stewardess 21
Kahriye Cami 31
Kahta 135
Kalkan 62
Kamazanoghüllari 138
Kara Ada 60
Kara Deniz 59
Karahanids 44
Karaköy Mosque 41
Karaköyunlü 140
Karamanids 138
Karatay Medrese 152
Karatepe 145
Karatey and Ince Minare Medreses 150
Kargamus, or Carcamesh 132
Karoglan 145
Kars 141
Kas 62
Kasim Aga 23
Kastamonu 156
Katpatuka 146
Kaunos 61
Kavaklidere Valley 53
Kaymakli 148
Kayseri 146
Kekova Island 62
Kemer 61
Keykavus II 150
Kirkor Balyan 42
Kitchens 21
Kiz Kalezi 130
Kizeltepe 133
Knidos 61

Knights of St John 60
Kokarkay river 62
Kommagene dynasty 135
Konya 150, 152
Konyali Cafe 24
Koprülü 129
Korkud mosque 62
Kose Dag 138
Kozan 130
Kresilas 55
Kroisos 53
Kudreddin Cami 154
Kul Hasan Çelebi 30
Külliye 14, 18
Kultepe 144, 145
Kumbet 137
Kusadasi, or Bird Island 56
Kuscenneti, or Bird Paradise 47
Kuthaya 141, 150
Kutsal Emanetler, or Treasury of the Sacred
    Relics 22

Labranda 129
Lade 56
Lake Aral 142
Lake Bafa 56, 57
Lake Manyas 47
Lake Van 138, 139
Lale, or tulip garden 24
Laodike 135
Lavra system 146
Lesbos 48
Licinius 11
Luigi Piccinato 16
Lycemachos 57
Lycia 59, 61
Lydia 48, 53
Lykos 59
Lysimachus 49

Maçka 44
Maeander River 57
Mahmud I 23, 44
Mahmut II 15
Mahmut Paşa Mosque 27
Mahmut Paşa Yokusu 27
Malatya 141, 145, 146, 150
Malazgirt 138
Malikshah 133

Mama Khatun Kumbet 142
Mamdoh Paşa Library 41
Manavgat 129
Manisa Ulu Cami 53
Manuel I 153
Manzikert 138
Marble Terrace 23
Mardin 132, 133, 135
Marmaris 56, 61
Marshall Plan 17
Martin Wagner 16
Mausoleum of Ahmet I 18
Mausoleum of Halikarnassos 60
Mausolus of Caria 60
Mecidiye Kösk 24
Medrese 25
Megara 9
Megarus 155
Mehmet Aga 18
Mehmet I 45
Mehmet II 14, 19, 27, 30, 32, 45
Mehmet III 33
Melendis River 148
Menemen 53
Mesruta ev 38
Mesudiye Medrese 133
Metropolitan Plan 16
Meyit 22
Michael Palaeologus 42
Midas 145
Mihrimah Cami 31
Mihrimah Sultan 31, 36
Milas 56, 58
Miletus 56, 57, 155
Minare Köy 61
Minber 25
Misir Çarsisi or Egyptian Bazaar 33
Mithradates 135
Mongol invasions 137
Mosque of Bayezit 26
Mt Argaeus 146
Mt Güllük 129
Mt Latmos 57
Munzur mountains 132
Murad I 45
Murad II 45, 46
Murad III 21, 33, 53
Murad IV 23, 33
Muradiye 45

Musavirler Heyeti 16
Mushki 145
Mustafa III 30, 38
Mut 130
Mylasa 58
Myndos 60
Myra 62

Naiskos, home of Apollo 57
Neandria 47
Nemrut Dag 135
Nesians 144
Nevsehirli Ibrahim Paşa 23
Nicomedia 11
Nigde 146
Nikogas Balyan 39
Nimrod 133
Noah's Ark 138
Nöbetyeri 22
Nurosmaniye 27, 42
Nusretiye 42

Olbrich 41
Olive Coast 47
Ölü Deniz 61
Olympias 49
Oracle at Delphi 11
Orhan Gazi 45
Ortahisar 148
Ortakapi 22
Osman 45
Osman III 28
Ozymandias 135

Pactolus River 53
Palestine 130
Pammukale 56
Pamphylia 59, 62
Panaghia Chrysocephalus (or the Virgin of
   the Golden Head) 154
Panaghia tou Melos 154
Panagic church 62
Panathenaic procession 50
Panayir Dagi (Mt Pion) 55
Parthenon 50, 51
Patara 62
Patmos 55
Patrona Halil 23
Pax Romana 55

Pehlivan Halil Aga 23
Peloponesian War 11
Pera 44
Pergamon 48, 49, 50, 56, 62
Perge 64, 129
Peristrema 148
Persian Wars 11
Phaesilis 64
Phidias 51, 55
Philadelphian Forum 12
Philetairos 49
Phrygians 145
Pinara 61
Piyale Paşa Cami 42
Plato 48
Pliny 55
Polykleitos 55
Pontic mountains 154
Praxiteles 56, 61
Priam 47
Priene 56
Princes' Islands 42
Princes' School 22
Procopius 9
Propalaia 51
Proust 28
Proust Plan 16
Pseudo-Baroque style 35
Ptolemy 49, 57
Publius Serviluis Vatia 129

Qizil Arslan 150
Qutb al-din Malikshah 150

Railways 15
Raimondo d'Aronco 41
Red Hall, or Kizel Avlu 52
Republican Period 16
Revan Kösk 23
Rhodes 60
Ribats 141
Rize 155
Romanus Diogenes 138
Roxanne 49
Rum Mehmet Paşa mosque 36
Rumeli Hisari 38
Rural migration 17
Russian emigrés 43
Rüstem Paşa 34

Rüstem Paşa Cami 33, 34, 35

Sadyattes 53
Safiiler Mosque 133
Safiye Sultan 33
Saframbolu 156
Sahaflar Çarsisi 26
Şahsultan 33
Sakcha 145
Saladin, Salah al-Din Ayub 130
Samal 145
Samsun 141, 155
Samsun Dag 56
Sandal Bedestan, or Silk Bazaar 27
Saray-i Atik, or Old Palace 19
Saray-i Cedid 19
Sarayburnu, or "the Nose of the Palace" 11, 19
Sardis 53
Sarduri 139
Sargon II 145
Sarik 23
Sarni Restaurant 24
Sat range 139
Schliemann 47
Şehzade Mosque 18, 29
Seki-alti, or pahucluk 38
Seki-üstu, or living area 38
Selamlik 140
Seleucus 49
Selim II 25
Selim III 15, 32
Selim the Grim 22
Selimiye Mosque 46
Seljuks 44, 138
Selucid empire 49
Semiramis 139
Şemsetin 32
Şemsi Ahmet 36
Septimus Severus 11, 12, 16
Severan plan 12
Severan walls 12
Şeyh Zafir 41
Şeytan Sofrasi 49
Shaminarmsu 139
Sheba 139
Side 64
Sigalik 54
Şihabettin Ilyas Bey 150

Sile 156
Silifke 130
Silk trade in Bursa 46
Sinai Peninsula 57
Sinan 18, 24, 29, 32, 34, 36, 46, 64
Sinan Paşa mosque 41
Sion 146
Sion Monastery 131
Sircige 15
Sirkeci 35
Şişe Saray or Glass Palace 19
Sivas 146, 150
Slavery 15
Smyrna 54
Socrates 47
Sofa Mosque 24
Soganli Dere 148
Söke 56
Sokullu Mehmet Mosque 24
Solyms 129
Spice Bazaar, or Misir Çarsisi 33
Split 12
St Andrew 154
St Basil of Caesarea 146
St Eugene 154
St Ignatius 48
St John 54, 55
St Luke 48, 154
St Mark's Basilica 9
St Nicholas 62
St Paul 48, 54, 55, 129
St Philip 154
Sublime Porte 13
Süleyman 14, 24
Süleyman the Magnificent 28
Süleymaniye 28, 29
Sulla 54
Sultan Ahmet or "Blue" Mosque 18
Sultan Ahmet Square 16, 17, 24
Sultan Isa Medrese 133
Sumela 146
Sumela Monastery 154
Sunnet Odasi, or Circumcision Room 23
Sur-i Sultan or Sultan's Wall 19
Suruhanids 138

T-plan mosques 27
Tagesken 142
Taksim 15

Taksim Square 44
Tanzimat 15
Tarabya 41
Tarsus mountains 59
Tasselled Halberdiers 21
Tea 155
Tekke of Mevlana 152
Temple of Apollo 58
Temple of Didyma 57
Temple of Serapis 52
Tercan 142
Terme 155
Termessos 129
Termiscyra 155
Thales 53
Theodosius 14, 16
Theodosius I 12
Theodosius II 9
Theodosius the Great 9
Theophylaktos 9
Third Court 22
Third Ecumenical Council 55
Thrace 49
Thracian Sea People 54
Tigris (Digle) 132
Tirisin Plateau 139
Tlos 61
Tobacco 155
Topkapisi, or Gungate Pavilion 19
Trajaneum 51
Trebizond 14, 153, 155
Troy 47, 144
Tudhaliya IV 145
Turbe 137
Turkish conquest 14
Tushpa 139
Tuzgölü 146
Tyche 55

Üç Şerefli Cami 41, 46
Üçhisar 148
Ulu Cami 45
Ulu Dag 44
Umayyad Mosque in Damascus 133
Urartu 139
Urfa 132
Ürgüp 146, 148
Üsküdar 11, 14, 35

Valide Sultan, the sultan's mother 21
Vaspurakan 139
Vedius Gymnasium 55
Venice 9, 33
Virgin Mary 54, 55
Virgin of the Black Rock 154
Von Hausmann 15
Von Moltke 15

White Gate 9
World War II 17

Xanthus 61, 129

Yakutiye Medrese 142
Yaprakhisar 148
Yazilikaya 145
Yemislik 39
Yeni Cami 16, 30, 33
Yeni Cuma Mosque 154
Yeni Kösk 24
Yeni Valide Cami 35, 36
Yenice Pass 129
Yeniçeriler Caddesi 26
Yezid 32
Yilani Kale, or Snake Fortress 130
Yilanikilise or Snake Church 148
Yildirim 45
Yildirim Mosque 45
Yildiz 40
Yokushyu 145
Yozgut 146

Zal Mahmut 33
Zal Mahmut Paşa Cami 32
Zeniketes 129
Zeus-Ammon 136
Zeyneddin Besere 150
Zeynel-Bey 137
Zilve 148
Zindjerli 145
Zuiciriye Medrese 133